*F*lesh and Spirit is unlike any other 'relationship book' currently available....You and your partner will never be the same.

Mark Gerzon,
author of *Listening to Midlife* and *Turning Your Crisis into a Quest*

A helpful guide for couples who wish to celebrate and deepen the sacred marriage of Eros and Spirit in their intimate relationships.

Aaron Kipnis, Ph.D. and Elizabeth Herron, M.A.,
authors of *Knights Without Armor* and *What Women and Men Really Want.*

Cover photograph is of "The Lovers," a piece created by Beatrice Wood, in the personal collection of Rue McClanahan (currently on loan to the American Craft Museum in New York City). In *Playing Chess With the Heart: Beatrice Wood at 100* (Chronicle Books, 1994), the celebrated potter writes, "We are here on account of sex, though we do not understand its force. There is glory when the sexual force is used creatively, when it is open to the magic of the universe."

Graphics by Gigi Coyle
Back Cover Photo by Elissa Zimmerman
Drawing by Jaquelyn McCandless

Flesh and Spirit

The Mystery of
Intimate Relationship

by
Jack M. Zimmerman, Ph.D. and
Jaquelyn McCandless, M.D.

BRAMBLE ❖ BOOKS

For information write to:

Bramble Books, 4001 S. Decatur Blvd. Suite 37-406, Las Vegas, NV 89103 or

The Ojai Foundation, 9739 Ojai-Santa Paula Road, Ojai, CA 93023

Library of Congress Cataloging-in-Publication Data

Zimmerman, Jack M.

Flesh and spirit : the mystery of intimate relationship / by Jack M. Zimmerman and Jaquelyn McCandless.

p.   cm.

Includes bibliographical references.

ISBN 1-883647-07-X (alk. paper)

1. Intimacy (Psychology). 2. Sex (Psychology).

3. Spiritual life. 4. Interpersonal relationships. I. McCandless, Jaquelyn. II. Title.

BF575.I5Z56 1998

158.2—dc21   97-40912

                                                            CIP

First Printing 1998

1 3 5 7 9 10 8 6 4 2

Printed in the United States of America

The paper used in this publication meets the minimum requirements of American National Standard for Information Sciences—Permanence of Paper for Printed Library Materials, ANSI Z39.48-1984.

Acknowledgments

First, we want to express gratitude to our children—Bruce, Leslie, Adrienne, Eric, Baki, Elissa, Elizabeth, and Richard—for living all these years with the mixed blessing of parents devoted to the path of relationship. So much of our vision has been shaped by our playful, challenging, and illuminating journeys together.

Much of what is authentic in our writing is due to the hundreds of couples with whom we have worked over the past twenty-five years. As we hopefully have served them, they in turn have provided us a laboratory for exploring relationship. Their curiosity, insights, and courage have been a constant source of inspiration.

We thank Hal and Sidra Stone, Emilie Conrad, Brugh Joy, Mark Gerzon, Aaron Kipnis, and Eleanor Zimmerman for their reading of the manuscript and helpful suggestions for making the material more accessible to the reader. We are deeply grateful to have such talented teachers and friends in our circle. To our dear coheart, Michael Hughes, we send a special word of appreciation for his many years of guidance and for introducing us originally to the wonders of the Imaginal Realm.

We also give thanks to Margaret Ryan for her skill at improving the cohesiveness of our presentation and her unerring eye for clearing up murky prose. Equally important has been her warm and generous enthusiasm for our attempts to communicate the power of relationship as a path of awakening. To Larry Bramble, our partner in publishing, we offer our gratitude for his editorial suggestions and for the magical way he produced a stylish book from a pile of manuscript pages.

Finally, we acknowledge with respect and unbounded gratitude, the unseen presence in our relationship who has guided, confronted, nurtured, and inspired us to describe the unlimited possibilities of two people loving each other. We are students of this presence—without whom we probably would have gone astray—and devotees of the revelations of spirit that have come to us through its patience, insight, and connection with the Great Mystery.

Contents

Part 2
The Soul of Relationship—
Third Presence and Sexual Communion

Part 3
The Harvest of Third Presence

Preface

Our journey starts with a particular woman and a particular man who have the remarkable experience of finding each other in the midst of a multitude of possibilities. They begin by listening to each other attentively in order to weave together their personal stories...

From Jaquelyn. I learned how to meditate around age forty, finally taking the time out of a successful psychiatric practice and the mothering of five children (from two marriages) to go inward and answer the call for change. As my meditation practice developed, it acted as a magnet for many new experiences that began to transform my life—most notably a new way of medical/psychiatric practice and a new kind of life-partner.

When I met Jack at forty-one, I saw him as an accomplished and manly educator-teacher with a well-developed, sensitive and gentle feminine aspect. He was able to dance with my more direct and incisive—sometimes confrontive—qualities without losing his own identity. From the start, I saw him as a marvelous helpmate in the task of raising my two young children, which he has done with generosity and devotion. My three older ones were eighteen, twenty, and twenty-one—and well on their way to adulthood—when Jack and I first connected.

The differences in the intellectual, emotional, and physical ways of expressing ourselves have always enhanced our powerful erotic attraction. This magnetism has been an abiding blessing for twenty-three years and has continued growing and strengthening along the rocky road of our sometimes tumultuous relationship.

As Jack and I began our spiritual journey together and learned to love one another more deeply, we became increasingly aware of the similarity between meditation and sexual union. The exquisiteness of the instant just prior to orgasm led us to explore ways of extending those ecstatic moments. At first, we naively called this practice Tantra, not fully appreciating the complex nature of this traditional yogic path. As our explorations deepened we used the term sexual meditation and finally *sexual communion* to describe the practices that emerged from our erotic life together.

Gradually, it became clear that extending the duration of sexual union created a powerful magnet for spirit to enter our lovemaking, just as spirit enters our psyche through meditation. By becoming increasingly aware on the "precipice before climax," the sexual communion practices we explored allowed us to enter altered states of consciousness together.

Two of the most fascinating aspects of our ecstatic travels has been the evolution of our visionary imagination and the ability to directly perceive the energy fields that infuse and surround our bodies. With the help of these transpersonal skills, we began to see our relationship in a larger context as *research* into the mystery of sexual love. Soon, we felt called to bring the practices that emerged—council, dreamsharing, energy exchange, and sexual communion—to those who came to us for counseling or joined the three-day intensives at the Ojai Foundation called "The Mystery of Eros in Relationship."

Eventually, the urge to write became irresistible. This book is an attempt to describe some of our explorations and discoveries on the journey of intimacy. We offer the material as markers for others who are called to explore relationship as a spiritual path.

From Jack. I met Jaquelyn in 1973, a few years after my first marriage had ended, at a time when my life felt distinctly out of balance. Twelve-hour days as a headmaster of an independent school consumed me. I had completed eight years of productive therapy with two eminent Jungians but, relationally, I was dying on the vine. Looking back, I see my therapeutic work primarily as an introduction to dream analysis, mythology, the nature of consciousness and unconsciousness, and the spiritual potential of the human condition. My relatively undeveloped sexual life was not significantly altered by this otherwise profound Jungian journey. My three biological children were sixteen, eighteen, and nineteen, and Jaquelyn's two youngest were four and seven when we began our relationship.

Jaquelyn's Freudian perspective and interest in meditation propelled me into a new world. Her refined mind-body awareness and sexual wisdom soon initiated me into the mysteries of lovemaking. Together we discovered the ancient wisdom that opening the heart allows spirit to inhabit the flesh. She encouraged—more accurately, demanded— openness and taught me how to uncover hidden feelings. Repeatedly, her unswerving directness and honesty cut through my more diplomatic but sometimes indirect way of getting at the truth.

Jaquelyn also helped me to become a meditator, both through direct instruction and the use of her visionary capabilities. After watching me prune and cultivate the many rose bushes that surrounded our house one day early in our relationship, Jaquelyn remarked "I saw a purple glow around your head while you were in the garden just now. I think you've been a meditator for years and didn't know it." Her observations shifted my perspective and I began to make a more vital connection to the traditional meditation practices we had just begun to explore at the time.

As our relationship deepened, Jaquelyn generously invited me to co-lead interactive groups with her. In that environment she taught me the power of intuition and direct truth-telling to help people awaken and transform. I returned to school to study psychology and counseling, but it soon became clear that our relationship was my major source of insight into the nature of the human condition.

Within two years of our meeting, my entire life had changed. Raising a second family gave me an opportunity to understand more deeply how our children can be among our strongest teachers. We started working with couples and conducting relationship intensives. My life as an educator took on a nontraditional, almost shamanic quality.

Jaquelyn and I are always eager to share what we are learning with others: family, friends, clients, and the participants in the relationship intensives we have conducted over the years. Eventually, the profound way in which books have influenced Jaquelyn's life led her to propose that we attempt to describe in writing what we were learning along the relational path. After recording many hours of dialogue about our journey, we felt ready to attempt writing about our experiences.

We worked well as a team: Jaquelyn held the flame that lit our visionary path and made use of her extensive knowledge of the literature; I became the primary organizer of our material and, most often, the scribe. As the collaboration progressed over a five-year period, our individual roles and the shape of the book changed many times. After a while, a more playful and unified voice emerged that had a touch of other-worldliness about it. Eventually, we came to realize that our relationship—or more exactly the spirit of our relationship—was the true author of this book.

Prelude
The Path of Relationship

Fear, anger, wonder—no matter
I am already in the river
Trying to stay upright
Losing my old self
Moving swiftly
Learning to follow
The currents of Love[1]

We hope you will experience the marriage of sexuality and spirituality more directly by the time you finish reading this book. As a culture we are just beginning to grasp the potential of *primary partnership as a spiritual path.* Historically, only a few have embraced this vision before, primarily because of the polarization of spirituality and sexuality implicit in our Western Judeo-Chris-

---

[1] The lines of poetry that appear at the beginning of each chapter are taken from longer poems, written by Jack as gifts to Jaquelyn on various celebratory occasions during the period 1992-1997. They are all previously unpublished.

tian culture. This split feeds the familiar paternalistic fundamentalism that has played such a large role in shaping our lives in the past. Only recently has the "degenderizing" of personal power become enough of a reality to provide support for men and women in creating truly balanced partnerships. This development has been instrumental in tearing down the barriers that have long separated sexuality and spirituality.

As a result, many of us have begun to discover that the desire to love and be loved arises from the same source as the yearning for contact with spirit. When the manifest soul is able to free itself from the prison of self-involvement, it reaches out for contact with its origin in the Mystery. But no teacher is more powerful than erotic love in stirring us from the slumber of self-preoccupation. This is why we believe intimate relationship offers so many individuals a promising path of spiritual awakening.

The path of relationship, like any spiritual orientation, requires a commitment of time, consistent attentiveness, and devotion. In the pages that follow we offer a spiritual perspective on relationship and a number of practices that have sustained and inspired us on the journey. We also offer stories about relationships—our own included—that we hope will provide nourishment and companionship along the way. Naturally, couples have to follow their own star and find a pace that suits them. There is no recipe or general program to follow. Our intention is to offer this book as an ally to others on the path.

Although we feel the heart of our vision is relevant for readers of all ages and circumstances, this book is written primarily for committed, spiritually oriented, mature couples. If either of us had picked up *Flesh and Spirit* when we were thirty or thirty-five, we might not have been compelled to finish it. Some readers may encounter doubt or resistance concerning our perspective on partnership—as did we, along the way. However, the vision and practices that emerged ultimately became an invaluable guide for our intimate life together.

If you are currently in a committed relationship, most likely you and your partner are veterans of many domestic adventures and have survived the shakedown phase of marriage. Perhaps you are both ready now to settle in for the long haul. If you already have a healthy respect for rough roads, washouts, and difficult detours—as well as appreciation for the breathtaking landscape along the way—then you should find this book helpful in negotiating the next phase of your journey. If you are seeking a new or more satisfying intimate relationship, we hope our offerings will provide a perspective that will help you to set your course and negotiate the mysterious terrain that lies ahead.

Our book focuses on heterosexual couples because that's who we know best. But everything we say about relationship and all the practices described (with a few obvious changes) should apply to homosexual partnerships as well.

If you are involved in a relationship, we hope you and your partner will be reading this book together, discussing the issues raised, doing the exercises, and creating variations or entirely new practices as you go along. Our experience suggests that one member of a partnership is drawn to a book like this and then tries to involve his or her significant other. That's a fine way to start the journey. But to get the most out of our approach, we strongly suggest that the "reading" become a shared adventure. It's a lot more effective and enjoyable that way.

We have found in our counseling practice that most of us "do" our relationships alone, without benefit of open and regular contact with other like-minded couples. Natural shyness, being too busy, the challenges of sharing our vulnerabilities with others, and the absence of a safe context in which to do the sharing seem to be the main reasons for this widespread pattern of isolation.

As a consequence, a great opportunity is missed. Couples therapy can be extremely useful in many situations, but it is not accessible to most people, either through lack of inclination or economic limitations. Besides, it is better to work on one's relationship before it goes critical, which is when the majority of people seek outside assistance. Getting support from other couples in a safe and welcoming setting (which we call a "Circle of Lovers") is an efficient, powerful, and inexpensive way to improve one's relationship. We urge couples reading this book and experimenting with the practices to move in that direction.

We are aware that the order in which material is presented in this book follows a "nonlinear" pattern. Most of the main topics arise early, are explored at some length, and then are returned to again (and perhaps again) for deeper and more thorough exploration. We feel this "spiral model" more closely parallels what actually happens in a relationship. For example, the discussion of sexuality in Chapter 2 provides the physical and emotional foundation for integrating the spiritual aspects of sexuality much later in the book. In between lies the material that naturally arises on the journey to this more expanded realization of a couples' erotic life together.

When two people enter a relationship, they each bring a complex life story. Naturally, these stories don't always fit together easily; in places they may even seem incompatible. If the relationship is to flourish, the partners have to learn how to reconcile their stories in a productive way. *Reconciliation* means learning to understand and accommodate each other's important attitudes about sex, religion, parenting, money—not to mention values, memories, images, and expectations about the nature of an intimate relationship itself. This *secular stage* of relating challenges each partner to learn the other's language and "personal culture" in order to build a foundation that will withstand the demands of time.

The terrain beyond the initial secular stage is full of promise and risk. Loving another calls for continuous re-evaluation of who we think we are and leads to the discovery of qualities in ourselves—both attractive and unattractive—that we never knew existed. As both partners become more skilled at facing the challenges of intimacy, their maturing relationship has the potential to inspire a level of awareness beyond anything either partner could have experienced alone. Partners *know* when they have entered this synergistic state of consciousness, because the love for each other and insight about the relationship are notably heightened.

The doorway to heightened awareness in a relationship can open spontaneously during the course of an ordinary day: a moment of unusually honest communication, a sudden wave of erotic arousal, or simply a silent meeting of eyes acknowledging the unfathomable mystery of love. How partners respond to these moments shapes the future of the relationship. If the moments are forgotten in the rush of daily life and not recognized as the seeds of a new way of relating, the continuing process of reconciling personal stories can become labored and joyless. As long as partners view their relationship as being exclusively a secular venture, it remains difficult to progress towards greater mutual acceptance and respect. For a mature relationship to flourish, inspiration and support beyond the secular domain is invaluable.

We have observed that such assistance becomes more apparent when the partners shift their point of view...

- to envisioning the *relationship as having a life of its own* beyond the two people involved in it; and

- to embracing specific relationship activities as *practices* requiring devotion similar to that of devotees on any spiritual path.

As this perspective evolves, a "Third Presence" makes itself known that transcends the secular nature of the partnership. This presence enters the partners' lives spontaneously—at first, often during a moment of realization that intimate relationship is a mystery beyond their mind's grasp. Some couples say that in Third Presence they touch the soul of the relationship; others talk about Third Presence as the spirit of their partnership.

Eventually, Third Presence can be experienced in many ways—as mentor, shaman, comforter, and bridge to expanded awareness. These manifestations become more tangible as the partners develop their joint "visionary imagination." Third Presence is awakened by the ability to *co-imagine* the wise and numinous quality of the relationship that transcends the two personalities involved. Particularly when the mood is lighthearted, we have come to refer affectionately to this source of spiritual inspiration simply as our "Third."

Our book is about developing practices that help couples recognize and manifest a Third Presence in their partnerships. Most of these practices were inspired by experiences in our own relationship that are familiar to mature couples: a startlingly honest exchange, a joint contemplative moment of great significance, a sharing of dreams that opens the door to visionary insight, and an experience of ecstatic sexual union in which the couple enter the mystery of wholeness. Although such times of heightened awareness are intensely personal, they also propel the couple beyond the confines of ordinary reality into a state of profound insight and compassion. The challenge is to develop practices that create a meaningful context for these experiences, invite their further occurrence, and establish an ongoing awareness of the visionary construct we call the Third.

The key to establishing effective practices and manifesting the Third is the development of the couple's visionary capacities. Since the beginning of human history, individuals have used their visionary gifts to create images of angels, demons, gods and goddesses, heavens and hells. Mystics on the visionary path develop the ability to relate to these powerful constructs by employing prayer, meditation, and countless other practices to enter what Henry Corbin calls the "Imaginal Realm."[2]

The path of relationship involves analogous practices: attentive listening and heartful expression, dreamsharing, joint meditation, intentional energy exchanges, and the conscious interplay of awakened eroticism and *visionary imagination*.

The visionary use of imaginative faculties is not to be confused with fantasizing or hallucinating. As many mystics have taught, the Imaginal Realm is, in fact, just as real as familiar material reality and, in fact, plays a central role in shaping our ordinary reality, whether we realize it or not. In particular, the more we have access to this state of awareness, the greater the part we can play in consciously creating our relational lives.

A "Transcending Relationship"

One of our most challenging tasks has been to find the right language to describe intimate relationship as a spiritual path. We wanted to find words that would convey the mysteries of erotic partnership and still be accessible to the growing number of couples already on the journey or at least prepared to begin.

We have chosen to use the word *transcending* to identify the kind of relationship that is our focus. What is being transcended is the collection of attitudes, images, and patterns which, together with the winds of worldly existence, create the familiar ups and downs of a secular relationship. However, transcending doesn't mean *rejecting*. Rather it means embracing secular reality but going beyond the dance of personalities into a realm where the erotic life of the relationship and the spiritual life of the partners become increasingly unified. A transcending relationship is built on a secular foundation but becomes gradually less preoccupied with

---

[2] *Creative Imagination in the Sufism of Ibn 'Arabi*, Henry Corbin, Princeton University Press, 1969.

meeting personal needs and reconciling individual differences. Although this transition can occur in the life of a youthful relationship, it is more likely to evolve as the partners live through the family- and career-building years and have more time for intimacy and spiritual development.

When the relationship moves into the transcending phase, a subtle but significant shift takes place. Gradually, the partners' interest in meeting needs and reconciling differences is joined by a natural desire to explore the Imaginal Realm. They still attend to the imprints of childhood, previous relationships, and the culture at large. But now, sufficiently freed from the tyranny of past patterns—and with the help of their Third—the lovers utilize their visionary capacities to *create the kind of relationship they imagine will deeply fulfill them and support their service to others.*

The dynamics of the relationship are slowly transformed as the partners strengthen their visionary capabilities. Eventually their practices allow them to enter the Imaginal Realm together to discern directly how the partnership is meant to evolve. Listening attentively in the expanded consciousness of Third Presence, they begin to formulate a joint vision that gradually takes the place of what each of them *thought he or she wanted* from the relationship.

This transformation can be difficult, particularly in its early stages, since the unfolding of a mature relationship resembles a continuous process of death and rebirth. What dies is the memory of old emotional wounds, long-held stories, and old images of who the partners think they are. What is reborn is a progressively less self-involved "I" that is interdependent with the relationship. This transition in perspective and attitude is analogous to the shift in human consciousness that was demanded by the discovery that the sun, and not the earth, held the central position in our solar system.

Partners manifest the emerging vision more and more clearly by continuously refining their relational practices. The practices and the vision are mutually transformative; both are experimental and always changing. Over time, every aspect of a transcending relationship grows more expansive and conscious: the forms of communication, the sexuality, the joint meditative and recreational activities—and, equally important, the differences and disagreements.

Consider sexuality, for example. During the secular stage of relationship, a couple's sexual life often helps to mediate conflicts of personality and the challenges inherent in building a life together. If the sexual aspect is satisfying, the relationship has a much better chance of generating good humor and a sense of well-being for both partners. Undeveloped sexual chemistry during the secular stage diminishes the couple's motivation to reconcile each other's stories, values, and cultural backgrounds.

Once the transcending path has been chosen, sexuality increasingly becomes a force for transformation. Together with the partners' imaginative capacities, lovemaking brings with it the realization of why they have come together. Erotic passion becomes a primary entryway into the true nature of the relationship and, ultimately, to Third Presence.

In the secular stage, the relationship primarily serves the sexual needs and desires *of the partners*. They come together for mutual pleasure, support, and the creation of family. In the transcending stage, sexuality primarily serves the needs *of the relationship*. Under the guidance of their Third, the partners come to see that their personal needs are best satisfied by dedicating their erotic life to further awakening and strengthening the partnership.

As the evolving vision is articulated more consciously and supportive relational practices are developed, the fruits of the partners' efforts can be further manifested through their individual and joint work in the world. *On the path of transcending relationship the partners co-create a partnership that is fluid, expanding, and whose conscious intentions include service to others*. The perspective of the couple on the transcending path ultimately expands beyond their personal relationship to include a vision of interdependence with other forms and aspects of life—human and otherwise, dark and light. By strengthening their imaginative powers and visionary capacities, partners gain access to a level of consciousness that allows them to see ordinary reality as only a part of a much larger universe.

We have deliberately used the word transcend*ing* rather than transcend*ent* in describing the path of relationship. Obviously the relational journey (just as the individual one) never arrives at a final state of perfection. How one travels the path is more important than how far one has progressed. As long as partners avoid the common tendency to take themselves too seriously, the passage usually brings ample discovery, healing, and joy to balance the difficult times. Ultimately—with the help of the Third—they find themselves in a continuous process of falling more fully and passionately in love with each other and the journey itself.

At the height of completing an early draft of the book, Jaquelyn made the following entry in her journal.

Right now, co-creating our writing is the harvest of our relationship with the Third, who is cheering us on, bound and determined to make it fun for us. The Third is teaching us to approach the writing like we make love, which is our favorite thing to do! At this moment, I can see Jack leaning seriously and so dearly over the word processor, using that brain of his to try to piece together our completely different styles. This book is so much like our relationship because it is the child of our union. The Third loves our lovemaking and now is pressing us into creative expression. We have finally reached a place in our lives where we have energy left over from our work in the world for a co-creative project beyond the "doing" of our relationship.

Part 1

Secular Foundations

Beginning the
Transcending Journey

One

Shadows and Light

How many times have I lost you
In the clutter of expectations?
Is that your hand behind
My mother's taffeta insecurity
Reupholstered when threatened by exposure?
Do I see your radiance hiding
Under my father's dark oak values
Worn from regular devotion?
The light in here is shielded
By yellow shades of fear that
Old familiar patterns will be broken

But it's only a matter of time
Before a long silky limb
Will compel my attention
Or the curve of your hip

Entice me to move the taffeta
Just a glimpse of your breast
Is enough to turn the temple tables over
And no parchment can veil your eyes
When they're back-lit with heartfire
There are too many memories in this room
Just a few pillows would serve us better

*E*very relationship, like every person, benefits from more attention. Perhaps you and your partner only have rare attacks of doubt that you will grow old together, but you still know there is room for improvement. Perhaps specific questions have arisen, such as...

- "How can we learn to communicate more honestly?"

- "We've been on a plateau for quite a while. How can we expand and deepen our intimacy?"

- "Our sex life is okay, but it's become patterned and predictable. How can we develop a more vital erotic relationship?"

- "How can we express our love for each other more passionately?"

- "How do we find a way to develop a more active spiritual life together?"

In other words, your relationship works pretty well, but it doesn't feel as alive as you'd like it to be. You want "something more" to be happening. Your commitment to each other is strong, but you want to go further, deeper. Short of some big surprise around a future bend in the road, you will finish raising the kids and continue helping each other do your work in the world. Still, there is something missing.

For some, the picture may not be so rosy. Maybe one or both of you have become aware of an ongoing resentment towards the other that is hard to understand and even harder to shake. Perhaps old disagreements persist and periodically erupt into major battles. Maybe you have caught yourself walking around the house cautiously wondering when the volcano is next going to erupt. You are well aware that real-life relationship is no bed of roses, but you wonder if yours has to be *this* full of brambles and crab grass. Perhaps you are about to make an unspoken agreement to withdraw from each other and not rock the boat.

Or perhaps the main problem is the lack of enough intimate time together. The demands of work and family fill your days and evenings. There just isn't enough energy left over to nurture the relationship. You have a modest social life and manage to have an evening alone once in a while, but mostly what you talk about over dinner or on the way home from the movies is predictable and not very inspiring.

Perhaps your lovemaking is becoming an endangered activity. Morning schedules are tight, both of you are tired by the end of the long day, and there are many chores and errands to run on the weekends. In fact, you may have finally accepted the fact that your sex life is not as juicy as it used to be. You are not sure where it's gone or how to bring it back. You get a lot of advice from various sources, but the patterns of life are hard to change. Maybe what bothers you the most is that your partner seems to be more or less satisfied with the way things are. Perhaps the two of you have different ideas of what constitutes a "good relationship."

Whether it's different values or expectations about relationship, lack of mutual recognition, difficulties in communication, loss of sexual passion, or just an uncomfortable feeling of being stuck in old patterns, it may be time to take a deeper look at what's going on between you and your partner and try to make some important changes.

The Transformative Power of Conflict

Taking the first step in awakening your relationship may require a change in attitude. Most of us find it difficult to accept the fact that the "shadows" in our relational landscape are a natural consequence of becoming intimate.[1] We tend to see conflicts, ongoing resentments, and frequent feelings of vulnerability as problems rather than opportunities for growth. We want our relationship to be working well—which, for many of us, means more or less harmoniously. More than occasional disharmony casts doubt on the viability of the partnership. When serious difficulties persist, we despair and want to flee rather than attempt to change relational patterns that seem so ingrained. We don't like to admit how often we wonder whether we've made the right choice of partner.

The root cause of such despair often can be traced to the ideal images of relationship we hold—ideals that are mostly unconscious. Relating is challenging enough in itself without making comparisons with some harmonious ideal. When we assume that a "good relationship" means a peaceful and amicable one, then trying to resolve a specific conflict is made doubly difficult. We have to work through our resistance to be "in the soup again" as well as give attention to resolving the particular issue at hand.

When the relationship fails to live up to expectations of harmony, a lot of time can be spent in judging and blaming each other. Especially when unexpressed, these expectations are often our greatest burdens, diverting us from using conflicts and differ-

[1] We use the term *shadow* in the Jungian sense to mean those aspects of an individual, relationship, or culture that are hidden or undeveloped, whether by denial, repression, or—most generally— unconsciousness. The shadow is not always "bad" or "evil," since "good" qualities can also be repressed or unconscious.

ences in perspective as gateways to improving ourselves and awakening our partnerships. A client put it succinctly: "I used to think that dealing with each other's problems was a burden. Now I see that the process helps keep our relationship alive and—I have to admit—actually fascinating."

"In the Soup": Expectations, Self-Images, and Dysfunctional Patterns

The challenge is to see intimate partnership as a crucible for transformation that effectively brings to our attention the expectations we hold about relationship, the self-images that we carry (often unconsciously), and the dysfunctional patterns in the way we relate. Making this perspective a visceral reality is the first step on the transcending path.

Where do our *expectations* come from? Childhood experiences, cultural ideals, and the deluge of media input have imprinted us with expectations of what it means to have a good relationship. There is no way to escape the effects of this imprinting. The challenge is to become conscious of the conceptions and assumptions we are holding, since they invariably get in the way of coming to terms with the relationship in which we are actually immersed.

For example, when a woman becomes aware of an underlying desire that has influenced her relationship choices—say, "I want a man very different from the man who married dear old Mom"—then some of her highly subjective and otherwise inexplicable reactions to her partner will become clearer. Awareness at least creates the opportunity of changing such reactions by altering expectations or even letting them go entirely. ("When I think about it objectively, there are several qualities Dad possesses that I would actually like in a husband!") Or when a man who sees himself as supporting the full empowerment of women realizes that what he *really* wants is a traditional wife who keeps his home fires burning, then he can begin to understand and possibly change his resentful reactions to his partner's growing career.

Lurking *self-images* can be even more difficult to bring to light than expectations of relationship. Most of us try to respond to the challenges of life in a way that satisfies specific behavioral ideals we've adopted as part of our self-image. How they arose in the first place may not be clear to us, but we still do our best to be the kind of person that fits the image.

Of course, at times our behavior doesn't match our self-image. When a misfit persists, we may blame our partner for "not allowing us to be ourselves," which usually generates a lot of confusion and anger on both sides of the table. We profess we are acting or feeling in a certain ideal way—for example, showing patience, flexibility, and tolerance—but our partner experiences something quite different. She or he sees us playing a very different role in the relational drama and doesn't appreciate being blamed for the miscasting. When our self-image and real behavior do not jibe, it is up to our primary partner (as well as close friends and co-workers) to hold up an honest mirror and invite us to take a look.

Obviously an intimate relationship is the most likely place to uncover *dysfunctional relational patterns*. The important question is whether partners want to *do* anything about them. There are a few basic choices. You can blame your partner, the relationship, or even yourself when dysfunction rules—in which case, you're likely to become even more ensnared by the patterns and end up wanting to throw in the towel and start fresh (or enter a monastery). Alternatively, if you are blessed by having a partner who is clear and loving enough to confront you, and you are strong enough to listen and restrain your defensiveness, then the blaming will stop and together you can begin to work on changing the patterns. Or you can break the log jam yourself by providing a strong mirror for your partner and hoping he or she will rise to the occasion. Either of these latter choices can be the gateway to creating that much desired "something more" that so many of us crave.

Viewing conflicts and dysfunctional patterns as opportunities for growth may sound like an invitation to masochism. Not at all. Obviously every difficult relationship is not supposed to continue indefinitely, however horrendous it becomes. Nor are we suggesting that *authentically earned* relational harmony is anything less than one of life's greatest blessings. What we have learned is that to begin the transcending journey one has to develop a *taste for trouble*, an inclination to probe the darker corners of self and partner. Otherwise, most of your energy will be consumed in continuing to act out the conflicts or struggling to hack your way out of the jungle of confusion they create. That approach doesn't work very well. As many wise teachers have said, "You can't solve a problem from the level of the problem."

An example from our counseling practice will illustrate the transformative power in directly facing the shadows in a relationship.

Unlocking the Truth

Jeremy and Teresa were married while still in college; the birth of two daughters, Tandy and Jill, followed a year apart, soon after graduation. Despite early financial struggles, Jeremy utilized his many talents to establish a successful career as an investment counselor. Teresa was energetic enough to maintain a warm and loving home, as well as doing volunteer work for several children's organizations and holding down a part-time job. Essentially, her life centered around pleasing others.

Just before their twentieth anniversary, anguish over Jill's persistent eating disorder brought the couple into counseling. Then in her second year of college, Jill had had little interest in therapy, her primary concern being academic survival. At the time, the older daughter, Tandy, was happily married and pregnant. Except for Jill's problems, the family radiated an aura of well-being and success.

When the topic of their relationship first came up in therapy, both Jeremy and Teresa denied that they had any significant problems. A few sessions later Jeremy mentioned that Teresa had told him she had paid a bill when, in fact, she hadn't. He said it wasn't the first time he had caught her in an insignificant lie. "Do you suppose Teresa's lying and Jill's eating disorder are related?" Jeremy wanted to know.

Teresa remained quiet for a moment as the question was explored—and then suddenly blurted out, "I've been living a lie for years!" She went on to confess that, during Jill's preadolescent years, she'd carried on an extended love affair with Jeremy's best friend Paul. "You were so involved with the business in those days that I was left alone taking care of the kids all the time," she continued tearfully. "I needed someone who was available and cared about me. Your long business trips gave Paul and me a lot of time to be together." Despite her affection for Paul, Teresa insisted she had always loved Jeremy and felt continually guilty about the affair. "But I couldn't stop it until Paul moved away," she said sadly.

Jeremy's shock turned into fury as he remembered the many times Teresa had refused him sexually during those years. In the sessions that followed, he accused her of sacrificing their relationship and the children to her emotional and sexual needs. To keep their communication open, they were encouraged to engage in regular "councils," during which each would take turns speaking honestly and without interruption.

The next few months were filled with tumultuous dialogues, virtually on a daily basis. During this period Jeremy admitted to having had several brief affairs during his business trips that were usually associated with drinking and drugs. He also confessed to a longstanding and intermittently active intimate relationship with one of his clients who had been Teresa's good friend. Needless to say, Teresa was outraged that Jeremy had accused *her* of indulging her needs and quickly confronted him with this double standard.

He insisted passionately it was Teresa he really loved. "I wasn't getting enough love at home," he argued defensively.

Caught by the long-suppressed shadows in their relationship, Teresa and Jeremy hurled angry accusations at each other day after day. For a while Jeremy threatened to leave, but he soon saw that his own behavior hardly warranted the self-righteous posture he had adopted. Besides, divorce was really not an option because of the couple's Catholicism, even though neither of them practiced their faith. In addition, the financial complications of separation and the thought of having to deal with their families of origin, both of whom were prominent in the community, filled them with dread.

But the main force keeping Teresa and Jeremy together was a growing recognition of their love for each other, inspired by the new honesty and release of long-held emotional tension. Even before their anger subsided and the slow process of forgiveness had begun, their sexual life caught fire in a way that surpassed anything they had experienced before. To their surprise, each of the many after-shocks that followed the original disclosures brought new love and increased sexual attraction.

Jeremy and Teresa set themselves the task of challenging even the slightest fabrication on each other's part. Teresa committed to being more direct in *all* her communications, whether that pleased people or not. Jeremy ended his long affair, cut way back on his drinking, and stopped using other drugs entirely.

Since Jill attended a local college and lived at home during this tumultuous period, she became involved in her parents' painful transformation. Her new role as witness, confidante, and adviser brought her closer to both of them, particularly Teresa, with whom she began to develop a new woman-to-woman intimacy. For the first time Jill became interested in her own therapy, which helped slowly to extricate her from the intensity of her parents' life. Finally she left home of her own accord and moved in with a girlfriend. Her eating disorder and academic problems slowly disappeared.

Most of us are loath to give up our expectations and old patterns of relating without a major battle. The stakes are high in a primary relationship and fear of change is a natural consequence. It's easy to pull the wool over our own eyes. Sometimes it takes an undeniable crisis in the family, as it did with Teresa and Jeremy. Are there other ways to hold true to the vision of relationships as a crucible for transformation?

✺

Council

To explore and maintain a transformative vision of relationship, partners need a safe environment in which they can speak openly to each other. Creating safety in intimate communication requires that each feels that the other is listening—not just hearing but actually listening *attentively*. Listening in this way means listening without being influenced by long-held beliefs, attitudes, or positions. It is an art requiring a strong commitment and lots of practice. No skill is more important in developing a transcending relationship. Learning to listen "devoutly" (as the Quakers say) or with "beginner's mind" (as in the Buddhist tradition) provides essential nourishment along the path.

We know of no form that is more effective for developing the practice of deep listening and honest expression than the *council process*. This ancient practice, which comes to us originally through our Western (ancient Greek) roots and, on this continent, from Native-American traditions (notably, that of the Iroquois, Lakota, and Pueblo Peoples) provides a means for communicating in groups of two or more. As we have been practicing it, council also incorporates a variety of contemporary techniques for enhancing the effectiveness of group dynamics.

Council can be used for sharing stories, articulating feelings, exchanging dreams, making decisions, resolving conflicts, co-visioning, and many other basic needs of groups and intimate partnerships.[2] The basic form is deceptively simple. The group sits in a circle and a "talking piece" is passed around from person to person. The piece can be as modest as a bit of driftwood or as elegant as a handcrafted rattle or old family Bible. Only the person holding the talking piece may speak, which he or she does as much as possible "from the heart"—that is, honestly, passionately, succinctly, and without attachment to the outcome. The rest of the circle sets the intention to listen with devout attention, beginner's mind, and without preparing their subsequent verbal contribution. The magic of council is created by open-hearted listening and spontaneous, heartful expression.

In a council of two (*dyadic council*) each partner speaks until he or she is finished and then passes the talking piece to the other. Creating an attractive centerpiece—a candle and flowers, for example—and preparing for the council with silent meditation, drumming, or listening to music usually adds to its effectiveness. At least an hour, and preferably two, should be set aside for the process and prior arrangements made to avoid interruptions. Otherwise, the pressure of time may inhibit the partners' willingness to take risks and share honestly. We have found that having a regular practice of weekly councils, with special sessions called as needed, is a good way to implement the practice.

You may be thinking, *Why do we need a formal process to just talk to each other? We can always find time to talk, particularly when we're not distracted by the demands of family life.* Perhaps. But council is remarkably different from ordinary dialogue, primarily because it gives conscious attention to the art of listening and speaking from the heart. In council something strong and heartful

---

[2] For a comprehensive introduction to this practice, see *The Way of Council*, Jack Zimmerman in collaboration with Virginia Coyle, Bramble Books, 1996; *Calling the Circle*, Christina Baldwin, Swan Raven and Co., 1994; and *The Ceremonial Circle*, Sedonia Cahill and Joshua Halperin, Harper San Francisco, 1992.

enters the interaction that evokes spirit in a way we only stumble onto now and then in the midst of ordinary conversation. Bringing greater attention to listening often leads to discovering how reactive and inattentive we've been in past dialogues with our partner. Over the years many of our clients and friends have made council a regular part of their relationship and family life.

Themes for Preliminary Councils

A couple can agree to focus on a particular aspect of their relationship in council—for example, sexuality, expression of affection, competitiveness, conflicts in parenting—or open the dialogue to whatever comes up in the moment. It is sometimes useful to pose a specific question to frame the dialogue. The following have proven useful in starting out with a group of couples during one of our relationship intensives.[3]

- Which of your partner's expectations of you feel appropriate for you to fulfill? How well do you feel you fulfill them? (Let your partner comment on your responses before answering the same questions.)

- Which of your partner's expectations do you feel are inappropriate? How do you handle these expectations? Can you imagine other ways in which you might handle them? (Your partner can respond to your comments before answering.)

Periodically, it is a good idea to plan more general *shadow and affirmation councils*, which can be framed in the following ways:

- What troubles me right now about you and/or our relationship is...

- What I am appreciating right now about you and/or our relationship is...

---

[3] We offer three-day "Mystery of Eros in Relationship" intensives at the Ojai Foundation and other places several times each year.

Councils on Meeting Needs

One of the ways we manifest our expectations about relationship is through a set of *felt personal needs* that may be conscious or unconscious, expressed or unexpressed. The usually unconscious assumption underlying all these needs is that the partner "should" meet them.

Some needs may not be negotiable—for example, "I want to have children." Some may be important but difficult to meet—for example, wanting your partner to be neither possessive nor controlling. Others are desirable but not essential—wanting your partner to share your passion for country music.

Obviously, the more conscious the partners are about each others' needs, the better the chances of having more of them satisfied. Unmet and unconscious needs often lead to critical feelings between partners, negative self-judgments about being "too needy," and eventually to doubting the viability of the relationship.

One way to avoid this debilitating pattern is to hold a series of councils to identify systematically the needs each believes the other should fulfill. As before, each partner can comment on what the other says before making his or her own statement.

- Needs of mine that are currently being satisfied are...

  "I'm blown away by how your read my mind sometimes, like bringing the cup of tea as we sat down to watch the video last Friday and putting the two brownies in my briefcase this morning. Those little things really make me feel loved."

- Needs I would like to see more fully met in our relationship are...

  "I need to hear what you're feeling—particularly about me and what's going on between us—*as* it's happening, not after you've been brooding about it for days and looking for an excuse to explode. I feel ambushed sometimes, like last Saturday when you berated my all the way to Tim and Suzanne's party just because I kept you waiting a few minutes. It took half an hour for me to figure out you're feeling deprived sexually, since I've been helping Maggie out in the evenings and coming home late."

- I am aware that I am having trouble meeting some of your expressed needs right now. These include...

"I've been feeling guilty lately about all those things I don't do, like calling you every day when I'm away. I get back to the hotel exhausted and then it's too late because of the time difference. And I felt bad last weekend when you had to go to your sister's without me. I don't know what to do when I get into one of my antisocial moods..."

- I feel you have several unexpressed needs that are not being met. These include...

"I saw the way you looked at Tina this morning. It made me feel miserable all day. I don't know what's happened to my sexual energy lately. I feel tired and uninspired. Maybe I should see Dr. Wallace. You've been patient, but this morning was hard for me. It would be better if you put out what you want directly. Maybe that would get me going."

Putting unfulfilled needs on the table in this direct clear way is the first step in negotiating the ways to meet them. The next hurdle is to realize that needs arise in large part from expectations learned in our family of origin and cultural milieu. This helps us to see that they may not be as important to our current well-being as we believe. If negotiations proceed in an environment of mutual trust, a transformation can take place. We begin to see that many of our needs are more negotiable than we thought originally and, more important, *there is a lot more to relationship than getting our partner to meet our needs.* This realization is a milestone on the journey to Third Presence.

For example, two of our close friends reported the following dialogue:

"It wasn't as hard for me at David and Lori's last night."

"Yes, I noticed. I think they've decided to stop cooing over the twins so much when we're around. They know how hard it is for us."

"Maybe. But something is beginning to change for me since that dream I had a few weeks ago—the one just after those two exhausting councils."

"The dream about meeting a band of lost kids and helping them to find their parents?"

"Yeah. I don't feel quite as angry about the whole thing. I've known for years how important having a successful gallery has been for you, although that hasn't made me feel any less pain— particularly when I see David with the twins or watch a father playing with his kids in the park. But since the dream, I've had the thought of becoming a Big Brother..."

"That's a relief. I felt upset after our last council. Your story about wanting kids since you were a teenager has stayed with me. I'm really sorry to keep on causing you so much pain. Maybe, in a few years, I'll feel differently."

"But the biological clock keeps ticking."

"Let's not get into it now. Just let it be."

Identifying Gender Roles and Stereotypes

That men and women relate in different ways is not hard to argue. What is far more difficult to assess is the degree to which these differences are innate or learned as a result of culturally imprinted roles and values. Despite our growing awareness of these gender roles, changing them is a slow process. A majority of the couples with whom we have worked are still influenced by traditional gender patterns and stereotypes.

For example, most women still take primary responsibility for the care of home and children (although there are a small but increasing number of exceptions in recent years). Women still relocate when their men are reassigned to a new job more than the reverse pattern. Families in which both partners work are now the rule rather than the exception, but the man usually earns more, due to the consequences of women's greater involvement in raising the children and residual discrimination against women. The results of studies in this area tend to be controversial.[4]

Apparently, in the vast majority of cases, the working woman still takes the major responsibility for the children and running the household. The man is seen as the principal wage earner in most of the relationships we encounter. Many men are still threatened when their partners bring home "a larger share of the bacon." Some women in the nurturing professions are uncomfortable with the increasing presence of men. Old patterns die hard.

Most of us accept gender patterns as a natural part of relationship. A variety of books, some widely read, have appeared of late

---

[4] Some show that discrimination has been all but eliminated in professional and management jobs. Others conclude that the primary challenge to women is maintaining job continuity and a level of availability sufficient for advancement, due to the desire to also spend significant time focused on family concerns. Still other surveys conclude that significant discrimination still manifests in setting blue collar salary levels and in the higher wage brackets as well.

that describe men and women's differing needs, goals, language, and ways of communicating.[5] Behavioral stereotypes abound: women share their emotions more directly and expressively, want more affection and foreplay as part of sex, and generally desire greater intimacy in their primary partnerships. Men want to resolve conflicts by logic and analysis, have egos that are more easily bruised, are more silent and orgasmically oriented during lovemaking, and tend to withdraw emotionally when they are upset.

Are these cultural stereotypes or are they the result of innate differences in male and female physiology? The first alternative— that gender-based biases are learned stereotypes—is given support by the increasing number of relationships in which stereotypical patterns do *not* apply or, in fact, may even be reversed. Basic qualities that have long been primarily associated with women— such as being nurturing, gentle, emotional, and volatile—are increasingly accepted and exhibited by men in a variety of ways. Similarly, traditionally masculine qualities—such as courage, self-sacrifice, competitiveness, and being preoccupied with power— can be seen in an increasing number of women in our culture. Although societal limitations still abound, the increasing acceptance of gay and lesbian relationships has also been a factor in changing gender stereotypes among heterosexual couples.

Despite the progress we have made in the past few decades, even a couple who tries to avoid gender stereotypes can be unaware of how *unconscious entitlements* still influence their relationship. We have found that many couples do not realize the depth of their own gender biases and cultural imprinting. Gender attitudes that emerge with some regularity in our couple sessions include:

About Men...
"Men withdraw and pout when you confront them."

---

[5] For example, *Brain Sex: The Real Difference Between Men and Women*, Anne Mohr and David Jessel, Bantam Doubleday Dell Publishing Group, 1989; *Theoretical Perspectives on Sexual Difference*, Deborah L. Rhode (Ed.), Yale University Press, 1990; *Men Are from Mars, Women Are from Venus*, John Gray, HarperCollins, 1993.

"Men never really grow up. It's like having another child in the family."

"Men conveniently become helpless or too busy when it comes to household chores or dealing with the children."

"Men always want to 'fix' emotional distress rather than acknowledge it sympathetically."

About Women...

"Logical thinking is more difficult for women than men."

"Women make better parents."

"Taking care of a household and children is not as challenging as running a business."

"Women never forget the wrongs that have been done them."

"The volatile emotions most women exhibit are a hindrance to making sound decisions and judgments."

Many gender patterns are maintained by *conspiracy*. For example, a woman might defer to her man on a regular basis when she feels his ego might get bruised, tolerate his self-preoccupation to an extent she would not with a close female friend, or take primary responsibility for the emotional and spiritual well-being of the partnership. Conversely, a man might take care of family finances in a way that infantilizes his partner and gives her little opportunity to deal with worldly realities, or patronize her volatility as endearing and "just like a woman" rather than challenging her to be more consistent in fulfilling agreements. Becoming conscious of such patterns is essential in laying the foundation for a transcending relationship.

But gender patterns may not be all culturally based. The second alternative—that there are innate differences in men's and women's brain chemistry—is supported by certain observable patterns in the education of children.[6] Behaviorists argue, however, that the brain may be responding in an evolutionary way to long-established biases in our society. The debate rages on.

Our basic view is that generalizations concerning gender attributes and patterns are less useful now than they have been in the past and probably a distraction from achieving real balance in a relationship. However, since patterns and roles persist (perhaps, in some cases, for physiological reasons), each couple has to explore this highly subjective issue on a personal basis.

Councils Facilitating Gender Balance

To assist in this exploration, we suggest that couples hold a series of councils that focuses on exposing unconscious gender imbalances and biases. Here are a few council topics we have found useful to start off the dialogues[7]:

- Describe the ways your parents exhibited stereotypical gender patterns. What were your feelings about these dynamics as a child? What are your feelings now?

- What generalizations about the opposite gender do you recall from your grade-school days?

- Can you remember a time in school when a "romantic" relationship got you into trouble with your same-gender friends?

- What general attributes of the opposite sex do you most admire?

---

[6]*Brain Sex: The Real Difference Between Men and Women*, Anne Mohr and David Jessel, Bantam Doubleday Dell Publishing Group, 1989. In particular, recent research supports the familiar observation that boys are more likely to be better at math than girls, even though the conclusion is arguable and considered politically incorrect. Several years ago, the newspapers reported a vigorous feminist reaction to the new talking Barbie Doll, which was programmed originally to say something like, "I have trouble in math class." Mattel reprogrammed her in a hurry.

[7]For other ways of exploring gender issues, both playful and poignant, see *What Women and Men Really Want*, Aaron Kipnis and Elizabeth Herron, Nataraj, 1995.

- With what attributes of the opposite sex do you have the most trouble?

- Describe your current gender biases and tendencies to deal with the opposite sex stereotypically.

- Describe any gender biases you see in your partner. Is your partner aware of them?

(Dialogues based on these last few themes may consume many councils!)

Movement along the path of transcending relationship is strongly influenced by how a couple handles the gender issues that arise spontaneously. Suppose, for example, an interaction takes place in which the woman feels unrecognized and responds with the accumulated anger of women long suppressed. The man could very well take such an attack personally, become defensive, and counterattack the woman's unreasonableness. But if he realizes that the extent of her reaction is far greater than is justified by the particular situation, and if he can also avoid crying "unfair!", then he can use the moment to recognize his partner— truly *re-cognize* her. That means thinking about her (and perhaps about all women) in a new way. For example, he might look for a hint of unconscious entitlement in his own position. Or he might seize the opportunity to explore his past lack of recognition of women and so contribute to healing his partner's gender wounds.

The consequences of such choices are important. It is essential to a transcending relationship that the partners' innate natures, talents, and desires, rather than personal or cultural attitudes about gender, provide the basis for communication, agreements, and conduct. A transcending relationship thrives on flexibility, freedom of choice, and a willingness to go beyond conventional patterns of behavior.

✙

Other Relational Practices

The practices we have found important as we have traversed the path of transcending relationship can be grouped into four overlapping categories: communication, sexuality, energy interaction, and dreamsharing. We have already begun our exploration of communication by introducing the council process. Sexuality will consume a lot of our attention in the next and later chapters. For those unfamiliar with "energy interactions" and "dreamsharing" we will introduce these practices at this point and then explore them more deeply in later chapters.

Energy Fields and Interactions

Although many of us believe that we are much more than just a physical body, much of the time we still act as if our "I-ness" stops at our skins. In reality, we are complex energy systems that extend indefinitely beyond our bodies and interact on nonmaterial levels with others and the surrounding environment in ways that usually escape our perception and understanding.

According to teachings from such traditions as Tantra, Kabala, and alchemy, a "bio-electrical" energy field surrounds and interpenetrates the human physical form, creating what is called the *etheric energy field*.[8] This energy field, which is not visible to most people, consists of an interactive pattern of bio- electrical flows arising primarily from seven anatomical centers called *chakras* (Sanskrit for "wheels of energy"). These major centers (innumerable secondary centers exist throughout the field as well) are focal points of energy located primarily along an axis that is parallel to

---

[8] We are forever indebted to W. Brugh Joy who first introduced us to the possibility of actually perceiving the chakras of esoteric human anatomy. See *Joy's Way*, W. Brugh Joy, Tarcher (Putnam), 1978. Through a process of field palpation he called *scanning*, Dr. Joy explored the etheric field of the body and applied his findings to both spiritual development and healing. Our investigation of energy fields became an important means for understanding sexual energy and other energy interactions between partners.

the spine. The chakras provide linkages or channels between the physical and etheric energy bodies, as well as serving many other functions in esoteric anatomy. Many writers refer to the human etheric field as the subtle body; we will use both terms interchangeably.

Couples taking the transcending path of relationship are greatly assisted by becoming aware of the ways in which their energy fields interact, whether they are in physical contact or not. This awareness provides the foundation for many of the practices we will be describing later. At this point we only want to introduce the chakral system and talk a little about the subtle body.

In the Eastern yogic tradition the chakras are seen as centers of awareness that connect the physical and etheric bodies. As such, they provide a conscious meeting place for the imaginal and material worlds.[9] By altering the energy of the various centers, we can transform our field—which, in turn, changes our perceptions, sense of well-being, and even our level of health. When intimate partners develop this capability, they can consciously explore and change their *joint field* in ways that profoundly affect the relationship. This is the basic intention of many of the practices along the transcending path, particularly those that play a central role in expanding the couple's erotic life.

In helping many people, over the years, learn how to use their hands to perceive or *scan* their partner's subtle body, we have found that the first step in overcoming the skeptical mind and resulting inability to detect energy is to image the field vividly. This is accomplished by giving trainees a "map" that describes the field in some detail and asking them to compare this image with their scanning experiences. Success follows invariably with regular

---

[9] Lama Anagarika Govinda taught that the great secret of Tantric yoga consists in experiencing reality on different planes of consciousness simultaneously. He called this "multidimensional consciousness" and pointed out that the various planes do not exist as separate layers but rather as interpenetrating levels of awareness that include the all-pervading consciousness of our visible, physical body. See *Foundations of Tibetan Mysticism*, Lama Anagarika Govinda, Weiser, 1973.

practice. The scanner also becomes aware of his or her own subtle body as the partner's field is being explored. For many, it feels at first as if a new aspect of themselves has been activated. But a realization soon follows that the subtle body has always been present; it is only the awareness that is new. Some remember that they felt it in childhood or, later in life, during moments of happiness, spontaneous creativity, or heightened sexual arousal. We will see in subsequent chapters how to make changes in one's subtle body and the joint field of the relationship through meditation, breathing, and visualization.

Dreamsharing

Dreams play a fundamental role in our psychic lives, restoring balance and literally maintaining our sanity, whether we remember them or not. Because of their ability to surmount the censoring apparatus of our egoic consciousness, they offer teachings, insights, and challenges from the deeper layers of the psyche. Dreams are, by nature, both personal and transpersonal: they speak the language of the personal unconscious as well as revealing the collective roots of the human condition. For many of us, dreaming is the most accessible state of non-ordinary consciousness, which makes working with dreams a natural ally of a transcending relationship.

As we will discover, partners' dreamstates and their ability to enter Third Presence are closely related. Being able to "read" our dreams and feel at home in the reality of Third Presence are similar capabilities. Sharing dreams prepares partners to encounter Third Presence together.

When sharing dreams becomes a relational practice, dreaming itself becomes more interactive. The practice can be both a profound dyadic meditation and a productive agenda for dyadic council. Sharing dreams also heightens intimacy in a way that prepares partners for the mysteries of sexual communion.

Two
Building a Sexual Foundation

Silky, wild, golden spirit
I love you
My mind will never penetrate your mystery
Only our bodies can unravel
The secrets of transformation
Playing in our lovers' laboratory

*P*sychological advances during the last hundred years have shed a little light on the mystery of falling in love. The process of *projection*, how we make *object choices* (the people we are drawn to), and the prodigious power of culture to plant images in our mind are now familiar attempts to explain how humans become attracted to each other.

From a Freudian perspective, for example, sexual chemistry is rooted in the strong bonding to the mother and/or father that begins with birth. For the most part unbeknownst to us, this bonding creates a pattern in our psyches that influences the way we connect with people throughout our lives. When this fundamental pattern is activated later on, often accompanied by inexplicably strong feelings, we may find ourselves powerfully attracted to someone, even before we know him or her very well at all. This *transference* of early imprinted experience—whether it be to a potential lover, teacher, or therapist—plays a fundamental role in determining those individuals to whom we become sexually attracted. These object choices are made uniquely by every individual through a combination of imitating and rejecting what was learned about love in childhood. Consider our own story, for example.

[From Jaquelyn] The attraction I developed in midlife to Jewish men was seeded during my early years by a deep love for my Christian father who cherished the Jews as the Chosen People and loved Jesus with great passion. His physical affection for my mother was obvious to all the children; he couldn't pass her by at the kitchen sink without a kiss, hug, or pat on the rear. As a child, I always felt his love for me, but as I moved into adolescence, he had difficulty with my emerging sexuality and uncharacteristically pulled away. My initial attraction to Jack, which was unconsciously infused with images of Jesus, reflected all of these "father strands" (my father's name was also Jack!). When my father died shortly before I met Jack, his last message to me was, "No matter what else you do, love Jesus with all your heart."

[From Jack] I developed a mostly reactive pattern of attraction as a result of my strong bonding with my Jewish mother (who died just a few months after I met Jaquelyn!). I was the first child, only son, and the apple of her eye. Her traditional marriage left her few opportunities for creative expression other than parenting until much later in her life. As a consequence, I received a lot of attention that was infused with my mother's disavowed needs and yearnings. When I was young, many of my female friends and classmates were Jewish, but falling in love with one of them would have been dangerously close to acting out the intense connection

I had with my mother. Although I couldn't have explained it back then, I was aware of the much stronger pull I felt to gentile women, particularly those who were committed to having a career. At the same time, a need to re-enact specific aspects of the early mother-son bond also contributed to my pattern of sexual attraction: I was drawn to women who felt I was special, just as my mother had.

Thus in many ways we were well-matched object choices for each other. Jaquelyn's sexual self-assurance and expressiveness drew Jack away from the strong mother connection that had limited his erotic development prior to their meeting. She was the epitome of the sexy, professional woman who saw him as special (even outdoing his mother with the Jesus association!). The unfulfilled parts of his mother were well-developed in Jaquelyn, so she extended his connection with the feminine. Similarly, Jack represented what Jaquelyn's father had yearned to be: one of the "Chosen People." To be with him gave her a sense of being chosen herself and resolved the pain of her father's withdrawal when she had begun to awaken sexually.

We are a good example of how childhood imprinting often creates strong *polar chemistry: the tendancy to seek in another what is missing in ourselves.* The pull is particularly strong when the polarity is unconscious, which it generally is, at least during the early adult years. The resulting projection significantly influences our chemistry with others, not only sexually, of course. When the projective process is sufficiently mutual—that is, when two people accept each other's projections enough to overcome whatever resistance they may have to starting a relationship—a strong erotic bond is established and the journey begins.

Subjective Sexual Chemistry

In addition to the important influence of parents on our lifelong patterns of attraction, there are basic biological and cultural forces as well. For example, some people are drawn to partners who they feel possess exemplary genetic stock: physical beauty, health, intelligence, desirable family roots, etc. This pull seems to be more instinctual than conscious in some people (having to do with survival and propagation), yet it can be so strong that it overwhelms common sense and even previously made decisions not to conceive. We know of several couples whose relationships were quite unstable but who became pregnant primarily because one of the partners wanted to propagate his or her "line" and deemed the other a source of "worthy genetic material."

Several familiar cultural forces influence sexual attraction. In contemporary America, many women find that a man's personal and worldly power, self-sufficiency, and wealth increase the chemistry, even when these attributes do not consciously play a major role in their value system. Analogously, men's attraction to women is shaped, usually to a considerable extent, by cultural images of physical beauty and sexual capacity. As a consequence, men's sexual attraction is more visually based, while women's depends more on an intuitive or direct sense of a man's talent and potential for power. These patterns are, of course, not universal and vary considerably from person to person.

Each of us blends biological forces, cultural values, and personal history in unique ways that determine our pattern of attraction. For some, a radically different cultural background or contrasting skin or hair color increases the chemistry. Others are influenced by voice quality, manner of speech, or the ways in which their partners move. Underneath it all lies the power of polarity: that which is less developed in ourselves tends to attract us in another. This polar force can be strong even in the face of enlightened self-interest.

An example of the latter is what we might call the *nice woman/ bad man pattern*. Typically, the woman in this situation has been strongly influenced by traditional values and has lived a somewhat sheltered erotic life. As a young and relatively inexperienced woman, she finds herself drawn to sexually dominant, "shadowy" men who treat her insensitively, perhaps even abusively, on an emotional level. She knows such relationships are destructive, but they remain compelling because they challenge her values and thus open the door to her own undeveloped side. Sometimes it takes several painful experiences (and, ultimately, greater aware-ness of her own dark side) for a woman to outgrow these highly polarized shadow relationships.

A similar pattern also plays a role in men's chemistry (the popular film, *Fatal Attraction*, provides an example). However, the nice man/bad woman form of the polar pattern is not played out as often, in part because being nice for men and shadowy for women has less cultural support than the reverse situation.

Objective Sexual Chemistry

The kind of chemistry we have been describing is highly *subjective* and at least partially unconscious. In a contrasting pattern that we call *objective chemistry*, each partner is erotically drawn to the other because of specific capacities they bring to the relationship. Objective chemistry usually evolves as a relationship matures, although it can also provide the motivation for starting one up, particularly in midlife.

The woman might bring skills in social interactions, the ability to organize financial priorities, and a capacity for compassion during stressful times. The man might offer the gifts of staying calm during times of emotional turbulence, providing material support for the family, or adventuresome contact with nature. Although subjective chemistry may or may not lead to a productive relationship, objective attraction generally provides a more dependable basis for a loving and long-lasting partnership.

However sensible objective chemistry may be, it is often diluted or even blocked by our shadow side. Desirable attributes in a partner may actually be threatening to the insecure, competitive, or jealous parts of ourselves. A still more difficult challenge is to recognize such "undesirable" attributes in ourselves—say, impatience, stubbornness, volatility, elusiveness, or excessive frugality—as *gifts*. At first these may seem to be burdens or even threats to our well-being; certainly they need to be moderated in the course of the relationship. But the patient, steady, predictable man has a lot to gain from the impatient, volatile, and unpredictable woman—and vice versa.

These more questionable gifts do not easily replace the positively experienced projective chemistry that usually ignites a relationship. Loss of projective chemistry leads to seeing our partner more objectively. Conversely, discovering our partner has some challenging personality traits tends to end the projective honeymoon. A difficult period of acclimation may follow before the questionable gifts can be seen as useful contributions to one's growth and development (if they ever are!). For a couple to be sexually attracted to each other *because* of such gifts is clearly a mature form of chemistry. Harvesting the rewards of objective chemistry is usually the result of a lot of hard work on the unconscious nature of the initial polar attraction. Consider the story of Susan and Mathew, for example.

An Exchange of Gifts

She had a passion for directness, honesty, and working out every conflict on the spot, day or night. He was an expert in rolling with the punches, working through what he called "knotty situations" alone and in his own time. Her intense confrontations exhausted him. He wanted to play more and let the knots unravel on their own. When Susan suggested they find a marriage counselor, Matthew said he wasn't interested. His goal was harmony and peace, which he thought were achievable if Susan would only relax and get off his back. She felt he avoided dealing with his procrastination, indecisiveness, and inability to express feelings that she was sure held him back in the world and also drove her crazy. These had diluted her original attraction to Matt, which was based on a lot of physical chemistry and his potential for being an excellent father and creatively successful in the world. He felt she was hypersensitive, close to hysterical at times, and much too critical of him.

Both Matt and Susan were unclear why either of them stayed in the relationship, since they were so dissatisfied with each other and their sexual attraction had waned. The polarity between them had "turned sour" and no longer provided positive chemistry. Without a major shift in point of view and more effective ways of communicating, they would remain too far apart to see what each brought to the other as a gift. On top of it all, Susan's biological clock was ticking away, but they had wisely put conceiving a child on the back burner as a result of their inability to be satisfied with each other.

Despite all these difficulties, however, they couldn't bring themselves to separate. Finally their conflict became so exhausting that Matt agreed to conjoint counseling, which began by focusing on how to fight more productively. That led to a short period of partial separation, during which they continued to live together but put their sexual life (such as it was) on hold. With the help of therapy, Susan slowly began to see that Matt's way of relating wasn't "wrong" and might even be a good balance to her more intense style.

Originally Matt had been attracted to Susan because of her beauty, intelligence, and his desire to have children—all of which had dimmed with her increasing disappointment and criticism of him. But her acknowledgment that he might have something to teach her helped him see that he might have chosen her for similar reasons—an idea he had never entertained before.

By committing to the practice of dyadic council, they slowly learned to listen to each other attentively without interrupting. After a while, Matt announced he had let go of achieving harmony between them as an overriding priority. A few months later they shared a spontaneous moment during a walk on the beach when the idea that their relationship had to do with an exchange of gifts became a felt reality. Gradually a new, less subjective kind of sexual attraction was seeded and they began making love again, now as a celebration of what they had to offer each other. Finally, two years after starting to work seriously on their relationship, they felt enough trust in each other to risk conceiving a child.

Councils on Sexual Attraction

To shed light on the mystery of sexual attraction, we strongly recommend holding occasional dyadic councils that explore each partner's erotic roots. The following areas of exploration have proven useful to us and many of our clients over the years.

- Describe your parents' sexual attraction for each other.

- What were your father's and mother's "types?" Was either of them the other's type?

- Describe your ideal sexual partner when you were a teenager.

- What kind of a sexual person did you want to be as a teenager?

- What forces shaped your pattern of attraction as a teenager?

- Describe the sexual attraction in your first few romantic relationships.

- Describe the sexual attraction in your most important sexual relationship before the current one.

- Describe the changes in the kind of partner you are attracted to since you were a young adult. Do you have an ideal type now?

- In what ways does your partner fit, and fail to fit, your image of an ideal sexual partner?

- Describe the type you think your partner finds attractive.

- In what ways do you fit, and fail to fit, what you believe is your partner's ideal image of a sexual partner?

These themes also make good council topics in a gathering of couples who meet to support each other's relationships—if you are fortunate enough to be part of such a "Circle of Lovers."

The Transformation of Chemistry

Changes in sexual chemistry are often associated with common shifts in family life. Some of these can result in a painful loss of attraction, although they all provide opportunities for the couple to create more objective chemistry between them.

Sexual chemistry often diminishes after the *birth of the couple's first child*. The strong bond between mother and child redirects her libido, particularly if she is nursing. Some men experience this bond as all-consuming and feel they have lost their wives to the baby. Another factor contributing to the reduction in chemistry can be the man's difficulty in continuing to see his new "wife-mother" as a sexual woman.

Even a temporary lack of fulfillment in the partners' sex life can lead to displacement of erotic energy into relationships with one or more of the children. This in turn further reduces the chemistry in the primary partnership. As most of us have come to realize—at least, intellectually—classical *oedipal bonding* provides an underlying dynamic in every family.[1] Father/daughter, mother/son, father-son, and mother-daughter bonds are all significantly influenced by sexual energy deflected from the parents' primary relationship.

A significant shift of one or both partner's libido into *career* can diminish the chemistry between them dramatically. This is particularly true during periods of financial instability. A loss of chemistry is also often experienced during periods of significant *physical change or stress*—for example, major illness or surgery, significant gain or loss of weight, or viropause and menopause (although, in the latter case, the opposite can also occur).

The tendency of one or both partners to *suppress anger* invariably erodes sexual chemistry. Long-held anger and resentment can eventually block sexual activity completely. And, finally, the loss of sexual attraction both leads to, and can be the result of, *extramarital affairs*, or other sources of external sexual gratification.

Some relationships experience mysterious, long-term changes in chemistry that are difficult to connect with specific life events or family dynamics. Perhaps the most common of these changes is the result of a gradual deflation of a long held, powerful projection as in the following example.

A Shift in Chemistry

Martha fell head over heels in love with George, who was twelve years her senior, soon after they first met. She had always adored her father and, like him, George was intelligent, generous, and kind. Her father projection onto George was also supported by

---

[1] We use the term *oedipal bonding* to describe the pattern in which there are primary attractions between children and parents of the opposite sex and antagonistic feelings between parents and children of the same gender. These attractions and hostilities have erotic components that are invariably unconscious, at least to some degree. Primary attractions can also occur between parents and children of the same gender, even when sexual preferences are basically heterosexual.

visual and other sensory images, since the two men had the same body type and spoke English with a similar accent, having both grown up in Montreal.

After four years of relatively trouble-free marriage, their sexual life began to diminish in intensity and frequency, until Martha finally admitted to her closest female friend that George didn't seem as sexually attractive to her as he once had, even though she "loved him more every day." She was mystified and upset, as was George, who, as a sensitive and experienced lover, couldn't fathom why Martha had lost so much of her former sexual passion.

On a few occasions Martha had become aware that George reminded her of her father but had never taken the association very seriously. As she got to know her husband more intimately and *objectively*, the strong projection began to dissipate. In fact, George and her father were radically different in several essential respects. For a long while she remained unaware that she was disengaging her father projection and, as a consequence, losing the special feeling of "in-loveness" that had been so strong at the beginning of their relationship. It took many conversations with George and her female friends for Martha to appreciate how important the powerful bond with her father had been in shaping her experience of falling in love with George.

Even though conventional wisdom accepts the phenomenon, many couples have difficulty in handling a decline in sexual attraction from the early days of the relationship. Rather than a cause for alarm, despair, or separation, however, this change is often a natural characteristic of a relationship trying to evolve. The subjective chemistry that usually precipitates falling in love may have to diminish in order to initiate the transformation into a sexual attraction based primarily on an exchange of gifts. The widespread lack of support for this perspective in our culture (as communicated through the mass media, for example) leads many to end their relationship prematurely during periods when subjective chemistry is waning. This was not the case for Martha and George, who survived the loss of Martha's projection and eventually developed a more objectively-based sexual life together.

Orgasmic Sexuality

Generally speaking, a sexual relationship is considered "good" in our culture when both partners are able to reach orgasm, either sequentially or simultaneously. Simultaneous orgasm is considered a preferable goal by some couples, since it allows for the window of blissful surrender to be experienced together. Alternatively, a common sequential practice is for the man to bring his partner to climax, either through oral or manual clitoral stimulation, before he enters her. Then, after penetration, he reaches his climax while the woman is still in the "afterglow" of her orgasm or perhaps reaches climax again. The reverse pattern is also common practice for other couples. In some relationships all these alternatives are part of the couple's erotic life.

Mature couples come to realize that any orgasmic pattern, no matter how satisfying, becomes a deterrent to the further evolution of their erotic life if it becomes ingrained. Some avoid rigidity by adopting an exploratory attitude towards sexuality that leads to a variety of experiences—some planned, some spontaneous—each time the couple make love.

Our purpose in this section is to discuss a few aspects of orgasmic sexuality that we feel are particularly important in understanding the practices of *sexual communion* that follow naturally when the relationship enters the transcending phase. These include: autoeroticism, the nature of men's and women's orgasms, and the pattern of discharging tension through sexual activity.

Autoeroticism

In our culture, the bulk of early sexual experience occurs when we are by ourselves in the typically private practice of masturbation. This is particularly true for males, more than 80 percent of whom masturbate, with some regularity, into their adult years.[2] Despite greater cultural acceptance, many people still feel some guilt and a need for secrecy concerning masturbation. As a consequence, the majority of men enter their conscious sexual life through the doorway of autoerotic activities that are somewhat clandestine, both physically and emotionally.

Furthermore, young males typically use the same or similar images and fantasies repeatedly during masturbation. This tends to support image-based, projective patterns during later sexual activity. In lovemaking, for example, it is not uncommon for men to re-enter a world of masturbatory fantasies that involves either their partner or other women. In the latter case feelings of guilt may arise. In any event, although it may heighten physical arousal and be acceptable to some couples, autoerotic fantasizing can also distract a man from being fully present during lovemaking. These autoerotic patterns are partly responsible for some men having difficulty in overcoming self- preoccupation even when consciously trying to be more attentive to their partners. The tendency for men to get lost in their own sensations and fantasies during sex is a complaint we hear from many women.

In contrast, less than 50 percent of women masturbate by the age of fifteen, although that number has probably increased in the past few years.[3] Many biological explanations for the disparity have been offered, including the far lower levels of testosterone in women. However, cultural factors probably play at least as significant a role—for example, the lingering belief that "nice girls" are

---

[2] *The Merck Manual*, 16th Edition, Merck & Co., 1992, reports that the *cumulative* incidence for males is about 97 per cent. See also *Our Sexuality*, Robert Crooks and Karla Baur, Benjamin/Cummings, 1990; and "The Role of Masturbation in Sociosexual Development," J. Atwood and J. Gagnon, *Journal of Sex Education and Therapy, Vol. 13*, pp. 35-41, 1987.
[3] The Merck Manual reports that the cumulative incidence for females is 80 percent. However, as Zilbergeld states (in *The New Male Sexuality*, Bantam, 1992), "Although in recent years girls have started masturbating earlier and more frequently than in the past, the percentage of girls who do masturbate is far smaller than the percentage of boys. And the girls who do masturbate don't do it as much as boys of the same age."

not highly sexual. In addition, the attitude that women's highest priority is to provide men sexual pleasure is still adopted by some women (and many men), a directive that obviously gives women less support for the practice of self- pleasuring. Whatever the reasons, it is clear that female sexuality often is less grounded in autoerotic practices and, therefore, women are less prone to self-absorption during sexual activity—a pattern we have observed in many of the couples with whom we have worked over the years.

Although men's and women's individual masturbatory practices vary in regard to frequency, the use of fantasy-images, and techniques of self-stimulation, the goal of orgasmic discharge is almost universal. Thus, a strong connection is made early in life between sexual arousal and discharge through orgasmic climax. This connection creates a challenge for couples on the transcending path, since being able to alter the inevitability of orgasm and, at times, voluntarily *let it go* entirely is basic to the practices of sexual communion.

Varieties of Orgasmic Experience

One might imagine that the vast majority of mature adults would be informed about the nature of orgasm. Not so. Controversy still swirls around the basic nature of the female orgasm, for example, despite the fact that we live in an era of medical and biological sophistication. Politicizing the issue for many years didn't help either. We can walk around on the moon and fly by Venus, but many of us are still not clear whether a "vaginal orgasm" is fact or fiction. Poets write about the ecstatic nature of climax, actors can fake an orgasm realistically on screen (as do some of us in the bedroom), but an aura of confusion and misunderstanding still surrounds the process.

Orgasm is unlike any other human response (although a humorist once compared it to a profoundly satisfying sneeze). Clinically, it consists of a spinal reflex elicited through sexual stimulation that results in clonic contractions of various pelvic and abdominal muscles. In males this is usually accompanied by ejaculation, and in both men and women the reflex almost always brings intense pleasure. These sudden, rhythmic, and largely involuntary spasms of the pelvic muscles are triggered predictably by both physical and mental stimulation and sometimes unpredictably, as in a "wet" dream.

This rational description still leaves us in the dark. In fact, even on a basic biological level the nature of orgasm remains somewhat mysterious. The ejaculation of sperm serves the biological purpose of fertilization. However, since a woman's orgasm is not necessary for conception, its biological purpose remains unclear. Might *pleasure* be a biological purpose?

It has been said that "orgasm is what a man feels and ejaculation is what he does." In other words, men can ejaculate without feeling the usual pleasurable reflex, and they can experience the orgasmic reflex without actually ejaculating (as in certain Taoist practices). In his excellent review of the subject, Zilbergeld emphasizes that there are many different ejaculatory patterns in men:

> Most authorities have accepted the contention of Masters and Johnson that while women have several different patterns of orgasmic response, only one type of ejaculatory response is possible for men. We disagree with this thinking, having ourselves experienced different ejaculatory patterns and having heard from a number of other men that they sometimes have ejaculations substantially different from the Masters and Johnson standard. Sometimes the excitement before ejaculation is so intense that it in itself feels like a long orgasm, and the actual ejaculation not only doesn't add anything to it but is experienced as a letdown. Another variant seems similar in some ways to multiple orgasms in women—a number of peaks that feel like mild orgasms are experienced, with ejaculation occurring only during the last one. Still another pattern involves contained pelvic contractions far beyond the usual number and long after the last of the ejaculate has appeared. Such

contractions are accompanied by feelings of intense pleasure, sometimes as pleasurable as those accompanying the ejaculation.[4]

However, confusion and misinformation about the male climax pales in comparison to the controversy that attends the female orgasmic response. Freud threw a few logs on the fire by distinguishing vaginal and clitoral orgasms, suggesting that the former are characteristic of mature women because they require intercourse.[5] He associated clitoral orgasms with younger or less developed women, since this type of climax can be achieved through direct clitoral stimulation without penetration (and, of course, without a partner as well). Needless to say, this point of view was not well received by the pioneers of the women's movement, many of whom supported women's right to enjoy a clitoral focus or any other desired sexual focus.

These women, among many others, were relieved to hear of the extensive research of Masters and Johnson,[6] who refuted Freud and supported Kinsey's famous study.[7] They concluded that only one female orgasm existed physiologically, regardless of the nature of the stimulation. Their findings delighted a large number of women, since studies indicate only 30-35 percent of women regularly experience orgasm during intercourse without direct clitoral stimulation. Women in this latter group (who were interested in the controversy) had difficulty hearing that some of their orgasmic responses were illusory. These women have continued to report that a clitorally stimulated orgasm without penetration is more locally intense, while orgasm with penetration is diffused throughout the genitals and, in some cases, the entire body.

---

[4] *Male Sexuality*, Bernie Zilbergeld, Little Brown & Co., 1978, p. 126. Zilbergeld also discusses the widespread misinformation about withholding orgasm that arises in male sexual folklore. For example, he stresses that the condition referred to as "blue balls" or "lover's nuts" is *not* a typical result of withholding ejaculation, despite what many men believe.
[5] *Three Essays on the Theory of Sexuality*, Sigmund Freud, Standard Edition, Vol. 11, Hogarth Press (orig), 1905.
[6] *Human Sexual Response*, William Masters and Virginia Johnson, Little, Brown & Co., 1966.
[7] *Sexual Behavior in the Human Female*, Alfred Kinsey, et al, W.B. Saunders, 1953.

The battle raged on. About fifteen years ago, Masters and Johnson's work was challenged in turn by others, whose investigations once again supported distinguishing vaginal and clitoral orgasms—renamed *uterine* and *vulval*, respectively.[8] These carefully done studies concluded that the vulval response can be elicited orally, manually, or through vaginal penetration and involves rhythmic contractions of the *pubococcygeus muscles* (the muscles that control the flow of urine). The uterine orgasm usually requires vaginal penetration and is characterized by contractions of the uterus itself, without involvement of the *pubococcygeus* or, more generally the circumvaginal muscles. Stimulation of a particular area on the anterior wall of the vagina along the course of the urethra, called the Grafenberg Spot ("G-Spot"), causes contractions of the upper vaginal barrel and the uterus but not necessarily the pubococcygeus. Some women produce urethral secretions during uterine orgasm analogous to the production of prostatic fluid in men.[9]

A third type of orgasm, which combines the vulval and uterine varieties, has also been clearly identified. This "blended orgasm" varies from woman to woman and even from one lovemaking experience to another, depending on the proportion of pubococcygeus muscles, upper vaginal, and uterine involvement.

At the same time that clarity finally seemed to be developing, new research appeared that blurred the entire issue of distinguishing vaginal and clitoral orgasms. In this study, conducted by the Federation of Feminist Women's Health Centers, the clitoris was shown to be a much more extensive organ that includes erectile tissue, muscle, nerves, and blood vessels around the vaginal opening and extending down the labia.[10]

The mystery deepens. The nature of the orgasmic response may continue to elude objective description and understanding. In

---

[8] *Circumvaginal Musculature and Sexual Function*, Benjamin Graber (Ed.), S. Karger, 1982.
[9] *The G Spot*, Alice Ladas, Beverly Whipple, and John Perry, Dell Publishing, 1982.
[10] *A New View of a Woman's Body*, Federation of Feminists Women's Health Center, Touchstone/Simon and Shuster, 1981.

any event, what *is* clear is the need for women (and men as well) to stop making judgments about the virtually infinite variety of women's climactic responses. In other words, to each his own. If a woman wants to expand her orgasmic experience and feels she is doing so, all the more power to her. What is perhaps more useful for us to explore is how a particular woman's orgasmic response may depend on her partner and the kind of relationship they have together.

For many women, achieving a satisfying orgasm, particularly of the uterine kind, depends to a great extent on the man's willingness and ability to exercise ejaculatory control. Although this seems obvious, it wasn't until women's satisfaction started becoming an important priority in lovemaking that the widespread existence of ejaculatory control problems was even acknowledged. Now that male sexual performance has become more strongly linked to the ability to satisfy a partner, many men have learned orgasmic control and, as a result, have found that their sexual enjoyment increases as they prolong the period before climax. Sexual therapists report a high rate of success with men whose motivation to learn ejaculatory control is stronger than their resistance to extended genital contact (perhaps due to deep-seated fears and conflicts regarding women). In part, as a result of these changing attitudes and practices, many couples have discovered that prolonging contact in intercourse opens the door to stronger emotional bonding and greater erotic intimacy.[11]

In recent years, human sexual studies have repeatedly revealed the importance of the circumvaginal muscles in the female orgasmic response. The muscles of women who are nonorgasmic are usually weaker and more atrophied than muscles of orgasmic women. Curiously, childbirth has not been shown to weaken or atrophy these muscles except in the case of poorly healed injuries.

---

[11] Although research shows that most women are capable of multiple orgasms with continued specific stimulation, it is interesting to note that only 10-15 percent regularly seek that goal in their sexual encounters. The majority of women (as well as men) appear to be happy with a single satisfying climax each time they make love. See *Our Sexuality* (4th Edition), Robert Crooks and Karla Baur, Benjamin/Cummings Publishing, 1990.

Studies reveal that women with the strongest and least atrophied muscles are often older and have had more children.

Poor tone, atrophy, or underdevelopment of the circumvaginal muscles affect a woman's ability to achieve orgasm, either with masturbation or intercourse. Thus, evaluation and strengthening of this musculature is an essential part of women's orgasmic response therapy. An evaluation can be done by the woman herself and, when indicated, a strengthening program started—say, using the Kegel exercises.[12]

Increasing the strength and voluntary control of the circumvaginal muscles can lead to the attainment of orgasm for formerly nonorgasmic women and increase the intensity of pleasure for those who are already orgasmic. Women often find that strengthening and learning to control their circumvaginal muscles through Kegel exercises also increases their partner's sexual pleasure.[13]

Kegel exercises are useful for men as well. The base of the penis is surrounded by an elaborate network of muscles (the most important of which is the pubococcygeus) that is similar to the circumvaginal musculature of women. In most men this network is

---

[12] The Kegel exercises will be described in a later chapter. How they came to play a role in sexual therapy is interesting. In 1952, gynecologist Dr. Arnold Kegel used pelvic circumvaginal exercises to help women with bladder incontinence from childbirth injuries. His patients found incidentally that strengthening these muscles improved their orgasmic capability and pleasure. Kegel agreed with Freud's concept of vaginal orgasm and disagreed with Kinsey's conclusion that the clitoris was the primary key to orgasm. Masters and Johnson's research, which followed Kegel's and reached different conclusions, did not specifically focus on genital musculature. See "Sexual Functions of the Pubococcygeus Muscle," Arnold Kegel, *Western Journal of Surgery*, Vol. 60 No. 10, 1952.

[13] Women who have become dependent on vibrators to achieve clitoral orgasm often find it difficult to reach climax with penetration, since the latter typically involves less intensely focused stimulation. These women may never gain much awareness of their ability to exert control over their pelvic muscles. In fact, the response to a vibrator can be so powerful and rapid that a discharge reflex can usually be elicited regardless of the individual's visual images and emotional state. On the other hand, women who masturbate vaginally either with or without vibrators usually have a higher orgasmic capability with their partners as well. This is probably related to their greater awareness and interest in pelvic organs other than the clitoris. See *Circumvaginal Musculature and Sexual Function*, Benjamin Graber (Ed.), S. Karger, 1982.

weak because it is used almost exclusively during ejaculation, which means relatively infrequently. The positive changes men have reported from strengthening these muscles by means of the male Kegel exercises include better ejaculatory control and more pleasurable orgasms as well as more pelvic awareness in general.[14] In addition, the Kegels increase the circulation of blood in the pelvis—an occurrence of obvious importance, since enhanced blood flow to the penis is the physiological basis of erection.[15]

Taoist Jolan Chang calls the Kegels the "Deer Exercises" and recommends them for both men and women.[16] According to Chang, these exercises can correct many male sexual problems, including premature ejaculation, low sexual hormone levels, infections of the testicles, frequent wet dreams, and impotence.

As this kind of information is more widely disseminated, more and more couples will experience that greater pelvic awareness and the resulting ability to prolong sexual intercourse qualitatively deepen sexual intimacy. This understanding is fundamental to the erotic life of a transcending relationship, which involves a variety of methods for extending the duration of intercourse before orgasm, as well as offering the option of nonorgasmic lovemaking.

Sexuality and Tension Release

Sexual relationships are associated with both pleasurable and anxious feelings in our culture. Often, the remembered physiological, emotional, and mental pleasure from previous lovemaking propels us into the next encounter. The body remembers the heightened delight of contact and the neural/physiological state of arousal reached during sexual activity. For a few blissful moments while making love with our partner, we often feel whole—valued

---

[14] *Our Sexuality*, Robert Crooks and Karla Baur, Benjamin/Cummings, 1990.
[15] *The New Male Sexuality*, Bernie Zilbergeld, Bantam Doubleday Dell, 1992.
[16] *The Tao of Love and Sex*, Jolan Chang, Viking Penguin, 1977.

and valuable. Life has meaning beyond ordinary reality. Our images and fantasies are satisfied. All is right with the world.

But sexuality and anxiety are also profoundly intertwined. Despite the so-called sexual revolution, many people still report having received little useful sexual training when they were young, beyond biological, birth control, and health information—if they were lucky enough to get that. The complex feelings connecting sexual functioning, self-esteem, and the expression of affection are explored openly in only a minority of families and hardly any schools. Most young people still learn from peers and through the media, both of which are often sketchy and inaccurate sources of information.

Sexual anxiety takes many forms, most of which are related to the familiar fears about performance and desirability that abound in our culture. For young and even not-so-young adults, the models for performance tend to stress the purely physical aspects of sex. Many young men die a thousand deaths worrying about their genital endowment. It is difficult not to grow up believing that bigger is better. For young women, the cultural norms for being sexually attractive are based to a great degree on physical appearance (breast size, shape of legs, etc.).

Sexual desirability is one of the highest priorities in our culture. But when being desirable is so strongly dependent on one's physical attributes (over which we have only limited control) and achieving ideals of sexual performance (for which we receive little guidance), the anxiety level can become extremely high. If we factor in the complexities of cultural and religious attitudes about sex, not to mention the often confusing imprints from early childhood, it is not surprising that anxiety and tension become familiar companions of sexual activity.

Since this anxiety co-exists with the intense pleasure of sexual activity, the tendency is to move relatively rapidly into an orgasmic discharge, which simultaneously releases the anxiety and provides a moment of physical and emotional pleasure. Thus, for most people, *sexual behavior is influenced by an underlying progression from tension to tension-release*. This basic tension/tension-release cycle can be broken down into five stages: (1) a precondition of remembered pleasure intermingled with anxiety; (2) arousal, which increases both sexual excitement and tension; (3) a powerful urge to let go and discharge; (4) orgasm—a moment of physical pleasure, validation, wholeness, and tension release; and (5) the experience after climax.[17]

The experience after climax varies widely, depending on how the lovemaking progressed, physiological health, and a host of other factors relating to the dynamics of the relationship. A few of the many post-coital possibilities include:

- An ecstatic "glide" that envelopes the partners for several minutes and may even grow in joyous intensity before gently returning them to ordinary reality.

- A state of peace and well-being in which the problematical dynamics of the relationship are temporarily subdued or even forgotten.

- A feeling of sadness as separateness replaces the state of unification immediately following the orgasm. Almost every couple has this experience from time to time, but it is more common with couples who are actively using sex to compensate for poor communication.

- A feeling of being spent, depleted, even depressed. This condition is more common with men and can be chronic if the desire for orgasm becomes obsessive. As the Taoists teach,[18] a pattern of frequent ejaculation

---

[17] In our work with couples, we have found that these stages of the tension/tension-release cycle are generally more sharply defined for men. Among the many possible reasons for this are men's greater performance anxiety once lovemaking begins and women's less intense focus on the goal of orgasm.

[18] See, for example, *The Chinese Sexual Yoga Classics*, Douglas Wile, State University of New York, 1992.

can result in significantly lowered libidinal energy, particularly if the sexual activity is lacking in affection.

The pattern of tension/tension-release during lovemaking is amplified by emotional, physical, and mental stress not associated with sexuality per se. The more stressful our lives, the greater the potential for relying on sexuality in general and orgasm in particular as a means of stress reduction. Although the tension/tension-release pattern can be eased by various practices involving breathing, imagery, and meditation (see Chapters 6 and 7), significant change ultimately requires that we take steps to make our lives less stressful. These steps are essential along the path of transcending relationship.

Sexuality in a transcending relationship thrives in an environment that is experimental, nonjudgmental, languid, and not orgasmically driven.

Establishing such a climate may require releasing deeply ingrained cultural judgments about sexuality. Prohibitions against the full and uninhibited enjoyment of sex generate obstacles for some people and a rebelliousness in others that lead to boring or titillating sex but few deep expressions of conjugal love.

Part of the human fascination with sex is its power to bypass our normal censoring apparatus and plunge us into the mysterious and sometimes shadowy parts of the psyche. (In this sense, sex and dreaming are quite similar.) Unconscious oedipal dramas, hidden fantasies, and our most tender vulnerabilities can be touched in the heightened state of sexual arousal. Thus, sex can be a primary avenue for exploring the darker side of our psychic life. If we are inclined to disown the shadow parts of ourselves—as most of us are—then the revelatory aspects of sexuality will be denied us as well. But experience teaches us that anything disowned is further empowered. The denial and fear around sexuality make it irresistible in that tense way that is so familiar in our culture. Sex becomes compelling in part precisely because it is still seen as bad.

This pattern limits our abilities to create a sexual life that fills our relationships with the spirit and revelation waiting to be discovered.

Three
Stories and Dreams

Stories followed each other
Some playful, some disturbing
Always turning us towards the light
Guided by your brilliant instinct
For creating plot and character
I am learning to trust those twists and turns
Those surprises of your imagination
Like Ariadne, inspired by the labyrinth of love

There is an old myth, the essence of which goes something like this:

In the beginning each human was both male and female in one body, and the world was at peace. But after a while humans came to believe they were as powerful as the gods, so the All-Knowing Ones split people into two parts called "man" and "woman." The separation created a mysterious and profound yearning in each part to find the other in order to come together again and experience wholeness.

This story must be the granddad of all relationship stories! It speaks to the yearning we all have for a "soul partner" and suggests that this yearning is related to the desire for connection with the divine. As a collective image of relationship it plays a central role in a vast number of personal stories.

Each of us lives a personal myth, a bigger-than-life story, that we glimpse from time to time but may never know completely. As we become conscious of this story, it reveals the themes and dynamics of our life that give it a feeling of purpose and direction. When we are unconscious of our story, our life is more likely to seem rudderless and without meaning.

On a deep level, our personal myth is a description of the process of individuation and the awakening of the Self. On this level we tap into the culture's collective stories (even if we are not conscious of them). Elements of the archetypal hero's or heroine's journey find realization in every personal myth.[1] Fragments of legends and fairy tales appear in our dreams and visions of the future. As we become conscious of our personal myth, we begin to understand the nature of our spiritual journey and our reason for being.

On the narrative level, our storyline reflects the influence of our ancestors, the circumstances of our birth, the nature of the body we are given, illnesses and crises, how we learn, our sexual awakening, our relational and family experiences, the ups and downs of our personal empowerment, and our death.

---

[1] *The Hero With a Thousand Faces*, Joseph Campbell, Princeton University Press, 1949; and *The Heroine's Journey: Woman's Quest for Wholeness*, Maureen Murdock, Shambhala Publications, 1990.

The challenge is to enter our story *consciously* and, in so doing, go beyond it. This requires practices that help us to discover our personal stories and evoke the power of mythical consciousness. Then we can begin to understand the forces that shape our life and give it meaning. Entering the world of story, we become more like children again—open, curious, and trusting that we are on a purposeful personal journey.

No two personal myths are alike, although many share similar themes and events. When we hear a personal story that touches us deeply, the chances are it's because the story overlaps a lot with our own. The exchange of personal stories helps us step back enough to witness our joy, creativity, and passion—as well as our pride, self-involvement and despair—thereby keeping a foothold amidst the drama of ordinary existence. Sharing stories was probably the primeval motivation for gathering together in council circles.

A variety of familiar human traits deter the discovery of our personal myths. Rigidity of self-image, fear of breaking old behavior habits, and resistance to changing relationship patterns limit our insight and clarity. We continue being lost in our story. We can't see the framework within which we are acting out our drama. We speak our lines and perform the actions but fail to step off the stage for a moment and witness from the audience. Without witnessing, we cannot become conscious of our own story. And without the perspective of a witnessing consciousness, we lose the opportunity to make contact with our *storyteller* and so influence the outcome of our personal myth.

Some call the storyteller the higher self or creative principle; artists might call it their muse; devout Christians, the personal manifestation of the Christ; and Native Americans from the Northwest, Spider Woman. Interacting with our storyteller dissipates the feeling that we are an unknown puppeteer's *Punch and Judy* show. Our sense of self is heightened. The veil between the seen and unseen worlds parts sufficiently to reveal major life patterns and a glimpse of future choices. We are given the opportunity to affect our story and even make a few major midcourse corrections.

♉

Merging Two Personal Stories

The challenge of relationship is the creative interweaving of two personal myths. The more conscious we are about this process, the more likely is the relationship to succeed.

Partners in relationship are like two weavers working on the same loom, trying to create a coherent tapestry without having a clear picture of the final design. The collaboration usually creates a lot of confusion, conflict, and pain as well as insight, growth, and joy. The former arise from those shadowy parts of our story we don't want to see. One of the main reasons intimacy is so threatening is the fear that sooner or later our previously hidden wounds and dark nature will be revealed. The anxiety can be great enough to question why we sat down at the loom in the first place. Ultimately, interweaving our stories involves transforming personal values and expectations, altering underlying patterns of behavior, and exploring new ways to manifest spirituality in our lives.

Resonant Wounds

In the course of growing up, almost all of us incur deep hurts inflicted by family, friends, strangers, and the culture at large. Experiencing insufficient or highly conditional love, neglect, family breakup, the untimely death of a parent or sibling, rejection by a loved one, sexual or physical abuse, or chronic poor health can create what many observers of relationship have come to call psychic wounds. Just as a serious physical wound can continue to affect how we use our body after it heals, so can deep psychic wounds influence our behavior and worldview long after we have emotionally recovered from the immediate traumatic experience.

But our wounds can also be our teachers. Mythology, great literature, and personal experience all affirm that consciously embracing our wounds in the spirit of growth and self-healing is a powerful catalyst for creative and spiritual awakening.

When we enter a primary love partnership we bring our psychic injuries with us, often seeking, consciously or unconsciously, to heal them in the relationship. Some may indeed be healed, but others can remain hidden or even deepen, and there is always the possibility that new ones will be created. Most long-term, committed relationships experience each of these situations at one time or another. The challenge is especially daunting when the partners' deeply held hurts are *resonant*—that is, when the particular nature of each person's wound amplifies rather than lessens the other's. Resonant wounds make it extremely difficult for partners to participate in a mutual healing process.

Michael was raised in an emotionally incestuous environment in which he was the recipient of most of his mother's loving attention. The unconsciousness and complexity of this relationship left him with a devouring mother wound, whose healing required a primary relationship in which clear and honest communication was a high priority. Michael wanted to know *exactly* what was going on between Katherine and himself all the time. The absence of clear intentions in the relationship or not understanding *why* his wife was doing whatever she was doing could propel him into sudden bursts of anger.

Katherine grew up the oldest of five children in a family that concealed their uncomfortable feelings. Her parents had separated when she was young, which was traumatic for her. During the breakup, neither parent encouraged the children to talk about their feelings with others in the family. Keeping the lid on everything became Katherine's highest priority.

Katherine and Michael's wounds *resonated* with each other. He needed her to commit to working through the many ongoing issues that confronted their relationship. She felt he was too heavy and wanted him to lighten up. Their relationship often got stuck in a pattern of mutual dissatisfaction. She wasn't sure she could be with someone who wanted to process all the time. He had trouble trusting her love because she often concealed her negative feelings. They clearly needed to find new sources of healing in themselves or outside the relationship, beyond what they were able to bring to each other directly. This failed to happen and finally, after several frustrating and painful years, they separated.

Resonant wounds often create a destructive pattern of poor communication and mutual feelings of betrayal. However, a strong commitment to discovering and reconciling personal stories—even those that contain resonant wounds—can open the pathway to healing.

The basic ingredients of the reconciliation process are:

- Remembering that we each live a personal myth and being willing to explore it;

- Recognizing that there is also a *story of the relationship*, a larger story that interweaves the partners' personal myths and is to be discovered together;

- Developing an erotic connection that is strong enough to break each partner's attachment to his or her old self-image and overcome the fear of being fully seen.

The core of the challenge is to discover the partnership story.

The Nature of a Partnership Story

The story of a relationship exists on three levels:

- The historical sequence of events and overt patterns of behavior: *The observable narration of the relationship.*

    —ancestry and circumstances of birth

—early family life and education

—marriage(s), career, children, successes/failures, crises

- Level of underlying dynamics: *What the relationship feels like.*

    —emotional imprinting from the families of origin and the culture

    —influence of sexual chemistry

    —compatibility of the personal stories

- Archetypal level: *How the relationship functions as teacher and transformer.*

    —the influence of archetypal forces in the story

    —karmic implications

    —how the relationship helps each partner to discover and shape his or her personal story

Each of these levels, starting with the third, strongly influences the preceding one. Thus the archetypal forces influence the level of underlying dynamics, which in turn shape the sequence of events.

Most of us "know" our relationship primarily on the first two levels, which is why we are often in the dark about what's really happening. We identify with the descriptive story and how the relationship feels but are mostly unaware of the puppeteer "pulling our strings," ensuring that we play out the more fundamental story underneath. One needs some detachment to see the level of underlying dynamics and the role being played by archetypal forces. This awareness provides insight into the "why" of the relationship and what makes it truly unique.

Sometimes the archetypal forces arise from a specific historical context (recall the central role that Jesus played in Jaquelyn's initial attraction to Jack). Sometimes they arise as collective representations of the human condition—such as the wise old man or woman, the divine child, the trickster, the lover, the magician, or the warrior. In each of these instances the presence of the archetype influences the relationship story, much as the appearance of a magical person (for example, the fairy godmother or the magician-hermit) empowers and redirects the hero or heroine in a folk tale.

A simple example is a couple whose early marriage is characterized by a pattern of one partner withdrawing affection when the other's behavior is unacceptable. Then the divine child archetype enters in the form of a beautiful baby whom they both adore. For the first time they experience what it's like to love unconditionally and, as a result, realize their previous limitations. The presence of the child challenges them to love each other in a new and less conditional way.

The appearance of the trickster in a partnership story (coyote in the Native American tradition) signals that a big surprise lies ahead: the old patterns may have drawn the couple together, but now they are about to see that the ultimate purpose of the relationship is to make some big changes in their lives! When coyote is afoot, couples soon develop the uneasy feeling of being on unfamiliar ground. Someone has changed the rules on them.

For example, Jaquelyn's strong mothering instinct and sexual self-confidence drew her to men whose wounds required those qualities for their healing. (Her attraction to wounded males started early, protecting her twin brother from a critical father and then becoming a more important part of his lifeline when polio confined him to a wheelchair at the age of fifteen.) Jack's wounding clearly called for sexual initiation. His history of strong maternal bonding made him a perfect candidate for the "erotic priestess" role that Jaquelyn carried so strongly. A perfect match—and a perfect opportunity for coyote to work his magic. Jaquelyn did her job well. Soon the awakened Jack needed help in utilizing his newly discovered powers without getting into trouble. That uncovered insecurities in Jaquelyn that had been hidden behind the priestess role. Jaquelyn accepted the challenge to explore new territory. Coyote had interrupted the old storyline and sent the relationship off in an entirely new direction.

Each of the partner's personal story has a cast of characters representing intra-psychic forces or *subpersonalities*—for example, the hurt child, the critic, the pusher, the judge.[2] The presence of these "figures" strongly influences the dynamics between partners. For example, getting along with a partner's strong pusher creates an entirely different set of challenges from those that arise when living with someone who's hurt child appears with regularity.

Discovering the Story

In addition to each partner's archetypal nature and collection of subpersonalities, the partnership story is shaped by a variety of basic themes or motifs. From the psychoanalytic point of view, for example, relationship stories incorporate a completion of the romance with the parent of the opposite sex and the rivalry with the same-sex parent. Examples of relationship themes of the oedipal type include:

- An ineffectual mother controlled by her critical husband produces a daughter who has two basic choices: identify with the mother and form a similar relationship, or aspire to be the kind of woman who would have challenged her father and earned his respect.

- The same mother and father have a son who likewise has an important choice to make: identify with the father and find a woman with whom he can repeat his parents' pattern, or rebel and find someone who is strong enough to prevent him from following in his father's footsteps.

---

[2] For an authoritative discussion of the way subpersonalities function, see *Embracing Our Selves, A Voice Dialogue Manual*, Hal Stone and Sidra Winkleman, Devorse, 1985.

- A puritanical father has a daughter who promiscuously lives out his repressed sexual side.

- Just a few years before his death, a loyal and devoted husband confesses to his son that he has carried on a long affair with another woman and wishes he had left his wife many years before. The son, who has had great difficulty committing to any woman, begins to understand his own behavior and goes about changing it.

- A father who is not sexually attracted to his wife focuses his erotic energy on his daughter (but avoids any overt sexual contact). As a result, she remains aloof from any serious erotic relationship until her mid-forties, when her father becomes seriously ill.

- A woman who marries a much older man for reasons of security and prestige makes her son her primary object of affection. He in turn marries a woman much younger than himself who soon learns that "Mommy-in-law" always comes first.

- A previously affectionate father, afraid of being inappropriately stirred by his daughter's growing sexuality, puts a lid on his show of affection and pulls away. She is imprinted with this pattern and ends up marrying an erotically unavailable man whom she is always trying to "wake up."

- A woman who sees her sexuality as the primary source of her power but who feels unrecognized by her highly successful husband unconsciously sets up a rivalry between her husband and her teenage son. This competitive pattern is deeply imprinted on the son, who lives it out repeatedly during his early adult years by trying to initiate relationships with women who are already involved with other men.

There are also a number of *role motifs* that often appear in relationship stories.

The grounder and the flyer. The "grounder" is the more predictable partner for whom continuity, stability, and being "realistic" about the relationship's difficulties are high priorities. Stereotypically, he (more often) or she is less emotionally reactive, approaches problems more rationally, and is most comfortable dealing with the practical realities of ordinary life.

The "flyer" is the risk-taker, less afraid to rock the boat, and curious to see what will happen if the relationship is given a good poke in the ribs. Coyote usually speaks through the flyer, whose great fear is getting stuck (which grounders are more likely to do). Typically, a flyer is more volatile emotionally, less logical, and more accepting of change. Of course, no one is a pure grounder or flyer, but one of the two basic tendencies is dominant in most people.

Generally speaking, flyers are attracted to grounders, and vice versa. This arrangement permits a balance of stability and movement that can work well for many years. However, for the partnership to enter the transcending phase, the partners need to become conscious of their grounder/flyer pattern and experiment with exchanging roles. Ultimately, the flyer needs to develop his or her own capacity for grounding, and the grounder has to learn to fly. Too much reliance on one's partner for balance, particularly if the pattern is unconscious, can eventually lead to rigidity and loss of chemistry.

The wooer and the wooed. This basic theme operates particularly during the early stages of a relationship, although some couples continue the pattern more or less indefinitely. The "wooer" is the one calling for more involvement, more intimacy, and a greater role for the relationship in the lives of both partners. Usually, she or he has a clearer vision of the relationship story, is less hurt by being rejected, and, in general, carries the pro-active principle for the partnership.

The "wooed" partner controls the pace of the relationship and is usually less secure in the arena of personal intimacy. The wooer/wooed roles may be reversed in different aspects of the relationship. For example, the man might be the wooer sexually and the woman socially, or the woman the wooer spiritually and the man the one calling for more physical involvement with nature. When the partners become conscious of their wooer/wooed patterns, they can begin to experiment with new roles and choices, resulting in greater spontaneity and balance in the relationship.

The caretaker. In this motif the man usually plays the title role. As the modern descendant of the knight errant, he becomes the patron and/or protector of the woman, often with a touch of the father-daughter story thrown in. Being the caretaker satisfies his need to control the relationship and keep his partner at arm's length—a position of relative safety from which to do his loving. The woman enjoys the many blessings of being cared for but avoids facing the challenges of self-empowerment. The incestuous undertones of this theme typically limit the sexuality from moving beyond the secular domain.

The strong sibling/weak sibling pattern. When a family has two brothers or sisters close in age, it is not uncommon for them to fall into a strong sibling/weak sibling pattern. The strong sibling is more successful socially and academically. The weak sibling tends to "not live up to his or her potential," becomes a concern for the parents, and generally carries a greater portion of the family's shadow. The stronger sibling is not always the older one. This pattern can significantly affect both siblings' adult relationships.

Hedda was two years younger than her sister Elsa and definitely her father's favorite. She was acknowledged in the family as the brighter, prettier, and more outgoing of the two sisters. Not surprisingly, Elsa struggled with feelings of inadequacy, which made Hedda feel guilty and led to her holding back her power when she was around Elsa. Although Hedda liked being the one in control, she remembered having a sad feeling of being alone when the two sisters played together.

In many subtle ways, Hedda was the controlling force in her marriage to Hans. In most of her premarital relationships, Hedda had been the flyer, although when she married Hans, some of her exploratory nature went underground, particularly after they started having children. During a conjoint therapy session, in which Hedda's relationship with her sister was the opening topic, the conversation wound up focusing on the couple's sexual life. Hans said he wanted their lovemaking to be more frequent and passionate. After beating around the bush for a while, Hedda spoke with great feeling.

"The problem is that when you invite me to make love, you're hesitant and unsure of yourself. I know I'm really in control, which makes me feel bad and turns me off. Sometimes, even after we get into it, I end up feeling alone...I don't know why that happens."

Her tears brought a long silence. After a few moments, Hedda was asked to repeat what she had said about feeling alone. Hans saw the connection immediately, but it took Hedda a few moments to realize she had used the same words just an hour earlier to describe her childhood feelings about Elsa. The recognition brought more tears and a compassionate hug from Hans. Then they started exploring how to break the pattern.

Beginnings

The way a relationship starts can shed a lot of light on the rest of the story. Our relationship provides a good example.

Our beginning resembled a fairy tale in which the hero and heroine meet at a masked ball and fall in love without knowing each others' worldly identity. We met in an experimental psychotherapeutic group for therapists, held weekly, in which Jack was a participant and Jaquelyn one of the two leaders. The ground-rules of the group prohibited discussing the conditions of ordinary life (marriage, children, occupation) or referring to anyone outside the group. Interactions were limited to sharing feelings, relevant dreams, and fantasies about other group members. Participants were not allowed to get together outside the group during the entire nine months of our meetings.

In this intense environment we got to know each other intimately on a psychological level, bypassing the usual preoccupation with personal histories, worldly activities, and behavioral strategies that are a familiar part of starting up a relationship. In other words, we began our journey by plunging into the second and third levels of our story. Supported by the group's mandate to freely share fantasies with each other, we developed a strong erotic attraction and glimpsed each other's essential nature before we knew if either of us was even available.

This beginning allowed us to avoid getting hung up on many of the differences in family upbringing, religion, and child-raising philosophy that subsequently became grist for our relational mill. The nine-month therapeutic "gestation period" set the tone for the kind of open and intense communication that has characterized our relationship ever since. We have often wondered whether we would have ever survived a more normal courtship, even with the strong sexual attraction we have for each other.

The archetype of the initiator entered early in our story through Jaquelyn's affinity with the the role of erotic priestess. Her extensive sexual experience together with our strong chemistry ignited a creative erotic life that enabled Jack to awaken sexually in a way he'd never dreamed possible. At the same time the shadow side of initiation was also constellated, although it took several years for that to surface. We refer here to the tendency of the initiate (in this case Jack) to attribute his empowerment to the initiator (Jaquelyn) rather than owning it fully himself. The feeling of dependency this engenders can lead to a rebellious and painful reactive period during which the initiate feels the need to prove he can be empowered on his own. That was a tumultuous part of our story!

Though she is well-grounded in her roles as mother and psychiatrist, Jaquelyn is a flyer: for her, adventure has always had a higher priority than harmony. Jack was converted to the virtues of flying as he slowly (and with trepidation) relinquished his well-developed role as grounder. We share these roles more equally now, although coyote still finds Jaquelyn's spontaneity an irresistible doorway through which to enter our story.

We are believers in James Hillman's eloquent thesis that an awakened relationship will inevitably go through periods that are "profoundly disturbing."[3] Ours has certainly been that. The challenge for the mature couple is to become skilled in the art of surviving profound disturbance!

Cultural Influences in the Partnership Story

There is strong support for mature, conjugal love in Western folklore and Judeo-Christian scripture (although much of it bears the heavy imprint of historical paternalism). According to some, these traditional stories still shape our relational lives, even if we have forgotten them or never knew them in the first place. For example, Robert Johnson has argued that the Tristan and Isolde saga still profoundly influences Western attitudes about romantic love (obviously unbeknownst to most of us).[4] In this myth, Tristan and Isolde's "intoxicated" love eventually leads to Tristan's exile and the death of both lovers. Johnson calls for a new myth in which romatic love is replaced by a cultural awareness of the virtues of grounding love in objective reality.

In recent times, ethnic diversity, cultural fragmentation, and the overwhelming influence of the mass media have diluted the effect of the old myths and teachings. As a result, contemporary relationship stories are less influenced by these sources of wisdom than they are by the secular patterns in our culture. Two examples:

[3] See the essay on relationship in *Blue Fire*, James Hillman, Harper and Row, 1989.
[4] *We: Understanding the Psychology of Romantic Love*, Robert A. Johnson, Harper & Row, 1983. In this myth (which is related to the Arthurian legend), King Mark of England is betrayed by his Irish wife Isolde and his nephew Tristan, who fall passionately in love with each other as a result of drinking a potion meant for Isolde and the King.

Happily ever after. Many early film and television romances followed the formula: "Man and woman meet, experience conflict, resolve conflict, marry and live happily ever after." Although most of us know better, the "happily ever after" part of this story still has the power to confuse our attitudes about relationship. If major conflicts are supposed to be resolved before marriage, then we are more likely to see disharmony after marriage as indications of major defects in the relationship. In fact, quite the opposite is true along the path of a transcending relationship.

We are usually drawn (unconsciously, of course) to partners who have some of the same negative qualities we experienced in our parents *for the purpose of working through the unfinished business of our childhood.* Thus a committed relationship inevitably stirs up enough trouble to fulfill this intention—hardly a "happily ever after" scenario.

Trapped ever after. Another contemporary cultural theme reflects the shadow side of traditional courtship. The story goes like this:

"Without announcing her purpose directly, a woman uses her erotic charms and related weapons to go hunting for a husband. The man is susceptible to her wiles and desires to share her favors but sees marriage as a loss of his freedom. The dance begins. The woman holds out marriage and creation of family as the price for sexual partnership. If she is skilled, she spins a web that results in the man believing he is actually wooing her. He struggles for a while but eventually surrenders his 'freedom,' which provides the story a 'happy' ending, at least temporarily. On the other hand, if her skill is limited or the man's resistance is formidable, the marriage never comes about and, after a possibly long courtship, they separate unhappily."

This familiar, dichotomized view of *marriage* and *freedom* is deeply rooted in our culture, particularly in men. The motif often plays an important role in the period right after marriage. For if a wedding marks the end of a man's freedom, then his early married years will naturally include mourning its loss. Not dealing with this directly (and, hopefully, with a little humor) can delay the partners from entering the more mature stages of their journey together.

We call a darker version of this motif the *black widow story*. In this variation (usually lived out unconsciously), the man sees the woman as capable of trapping and devouring him. He minimizes his chances of being consumed by avoiding deep commitment and intimacy. Challenged by his pattern of avoidance, the woman does her best to draw the man further into the relationship—which only confirms his fear that she wants to eat him up alive. Getting free of this story requires that the partners sort out the extent to which the woman is needy and insecure—and, therefore, "devouring"—from the man's pattern of hiding a deep fear of intimacy behind a negative image of his partner. The Don Juan myth offers a loosely related theme with the roles reversed.

Do we ever know how our relationship story is meant to turn out? The partners themselves cannot hope for total clarity. However great our perceptual skills, getting close to the truth requires witnessing from a vantage point that transcends the relationship. This perspective is provided by Third Presence. If our intention is strong and we are devoted to our relational practices, we are more likely to be blessed by glimpses of our true story as a result of an enlightening council, a dream, or some other moment of profound communion. Knowing our existing relationship story and going beyond it are ultimately mystical experiences. With the help of Third Presence, we can begin to transcend the story and more completely fulfill the relationship's promise.

Dyadic council offers a good way for couples to discover their personal and partnership stories, since the practice encourages detached witnessing more strongly than does informal dialogue. Obviously, soliciting reflection from other couples or individuals (friends, family members, or therapists) can provide additional insight. The councils can focus on a chosen motif, call forth childhood stories, or attend to existing relational patterns. In addition, personal and partnership stories can be illuminated spontaneously during any dyadic council if the couple has made their exploration a strong intention.

Dreams also help to bring an objective perspective to the exploration by revealing the archetypal forces that shape our stories. The regular sharing of dreams expands mythic consciousness, sharpens our perception of storyline, and encourages intimate contact with our storytellers.

⚭

Dreamsharing

Recent research into the function and purpose of dreaming supports what many who work with dreams have come to know through direct experience: *self*-awareness and awareness of *other* are inseparable. In other words, *we define ourselves through relationship*.[5] Dreaming provides each of us nightly access to the visionary consciousness of the Imaginal Realm.[6] It is not surprising, then, that sharing dreams is a powerful source of inspiration and guidance along the transcending path.

A regular dreamsharing practice helps each partner become intimate with the other's personal desires, fears, and need for balance. Since the normal censoring apparatus of the waking ego is largely bypassed during dreaming, utilizing information from the dream world eventually raises the level of honesty elsewhere in the relationship. Sharing dreams openly leaves little else to hide and helps the partnership to flourish.

One of the most interesting aspects of dreamsharing is to discover the roles we play in our partner's dreams. Some may be appreciated more than others, but how we "cast" our partner in a

---

[5] See *The Dreaming Universe*, Fred Alan Wolf, Simon and Schuster, 1994.
[6] The Aboriginal people of Australia refer to visionary consciousness as *dreamtime*. They see dreamtime as the historical epoch out of which the earth, animals, and people emerged, as well as a contemporary spirit source of nighttime dreams and visionary experiences.

dream usually reflects what's going on in the partnership. At a critical point in our relationship, Jack had a dream in which Jaquelyn and his "inner woman" or *anima*[7] fall into a passionate embrace. Jack is moved by this into a state of intense spiritual and erotic arousal. Casting Jaquelyn in this role suggested a major unifying movement was taking place on the archetypal level of the relationship.

Dream Practices

Although each couple eventually find their own way to share dreams, we have found the following guidelines useful in setting up a regular practice.

- Whenever possible, arrange the schedule so that there is time for dreamsharing in the morning before the day starts. Trying to hold onto the feeling-tone of a dream until the evening or next weekend's dyadic council can be difficult and frustrating. A willingness to wake up in the middle of the night to hear or share a dream often yields insights that justify the loss of sleep.

- When a strong need for guidance arises in the relation-ship or in either of the partner's individual lives, ask for a dream before going to sleep. This can be accomplished by quietly repeating a dream invocation, either out loud or silently, such as, "I am ready to receive a dream that will help my partner and me deal with our difficulties more honestly." Having a tape recorder or notebook and flashlight close at hand to record the dream provides practical support for this intention.

- Dreamsharing is usually best conducted in the spirit of council. Listen to your partner's entire dream, asking only for clarification of content along the way. Then invite your partner's reflections and associations before

---

[7] C. G. Jung's term for the feminine archetype in a man, which manifests as a woman in his dreams.

offering your own. Perhaps your partner's dream reminds you of one of yours or a story from the past. Finally, if your interpretive faculties are dying to be exercised, go for it without attachment to how your speculations are received. Even experienced dream readers can diminish the power of the practice with overly enthusiastic interpretations of their partner's dreams. We have run into this difficulty on more than a few occasions.

- Allowing for a few quiet moments after dreamsharing usually helps partners integrate the experience and plant seeds for the next round of dreaming. During critical times in our relationship, we have often been blessed by a long night of illuminating dreams interspersed with periods of sleep or meditation. Such dreamsharing can lead to a state of detached clarity in which aspects of the relationship are seen with relatively little distortion. At these moments we feel the Third's presence, witnessing our relationship with objectivity and compassion.

Co-Dreaming

As partners become intimate with each other's dream life, a variety of benefits begin to blossom. One is the simultaneous appearance of images or extended fragments in both partners' dreams. There are few experiences more intriguing than waking up from a dream and finding out that your partner has been visited by a similar vision. The synchronicity of *co-dreaming* can inspire great clarity, as the following story reveals.

Sabrina and Ted had been married, divorced, and resumed their complex relationship again when I [Jack] first started working with them. Sabrina had a long history of childhood sexual abuse, which continued to prevent her from enjoying an active erotic life. As a result of her devotion to exploring the complexities of her personal journey, she had developed a facility for exploring the non-ordinary states of reality that make up the Imaginal Realm.

In general, Ted was supportive of Sabrina's inner work and the couple counseling, although he felt more at home in ordinary states of consciousness. His greatest concerns were the absence of an active erotic life with Sabrina and her unstable health. She believed that a greater interest in our conjoint sessions on Ted's part and doing his own inner work would help heal her early wounding. Ted thought healing could be better effected through establishing a satisfying sexual life, getting remarried, and having the children he wanted so badly. For many obvious reasons, Sabrina was hesitant about becoming a mother. Periodically one or both of them wanted to get married again but were afraid to take the step.

During a particularly dramatic period in their journey together, I had the urge to shift my role from therapist to being a stand-in for their Third. When I explained to them what that meant, Ted was a little skeptical but agreed to give it a try. Sabrina, on the other hand, was delighted with my suggestion because of her general interest in relating to the Imaginal Realm and also, as a therapist herself, she was curious about the process.

After this experiment had proceeded for a few months, the couple was blessed with a night of dreaming interspersed with periods of great clarity. At one point Sabrina had a dream in which she proposed to Ted that he participate in a *menage a trois* involving herself and a woman who was under a dark witch's spell (representing her wounded self, we decided later). When she awoke, and before she had the chance to share the dream, Ted said he had "heard" her proposition while he slept (although at that point he couldn't remember dreaming) and proceeded to describe her dream with uncanny accuracy. In that moment, he *saw* their relationship story clearly. Despite his affinity for the role of caretaker, he turned down her offer, having seen that her healing was primarily her responsibility. A discussion of unusual honesty followed, after which they fell back to sleep.

An hour later Sabrina had a dream that directed her to heal the entranced woman herself. Obviously her "dream weavers" had heard Ted loud and clear. This dream was followed immediately by another in which Ted invited her to leave her house and join him. She couldn't accept the invitation, however, because it would mean abandoning her baby, who was very frightened (Sabrina's abuse began before she was two). Suddenly I appeared outside her window, whereupon she asked if I would be willing to take care of the baby so she could join Ted. I readily agreed, entered the house, and they went off together. We all agreed that I had appeared in Sabrina's dream as a stand-in for their Third.

That night proved to be a turning point in their relationship. A few months later, in one of our couple workshops, Ted spontaneously proposed marriage to Sabrina while they were being witnessed by the entire group. She accepted on the spot. During the wedding ceremony, Ted had a spontaneous experience of Third Presence, which made him feel connected to Sabrina in a new way. Third Presence became increasingly accessible to them from that time on.

Dreams of the Third

Sometimes an entity representing the Third appears in one partner's dreams. The entity is usually bigger-than-life, often androgynous, and usually cast in the role of a teacher, mythological character, or less often, someone the partners know (as in Sabrina's dream). The figure usually connects with equal intensity to both partners in the dream.

I [Jack] had a night vision of this type a short time after we began to recognize the presence of our otherworldly ally. The following dream conveyed the strong sense of reality often associated with big or so-called "astral dreams."

Jaquelyn and I were talking softly and moving towards lovemaking. Suddenly at the foot of the bed a nude couple appeared in an interpenetrating tantric embrace. The man was slender, with abundant dark curly hair; the woman's beautifully formed body exuded sensuality. We couldn't see their faces, but I knew we hadn't met them before. They were so real that I became afraid and, without thinking, grabbed my flashlight and directed the beam at them. The light moved them off the bed, but they remained in an embrace hovering in the center of the room. I was afraid of being in the presence of such powerful figures yet fascinated by the soft golden light they radiated. A voice inside the dream challenged me to restrain my fear and accept the reality of the spirit couple's presence. I struggled for a moment until my apprehension subsided and I was able to put down the flashlight. As I awoke, their presence lingered in the middle of the room.

The vividness of the dream stayed with me for a long time. A week later we received a synchronistic gift of a beautiful tantric Tanka, which hung on our bedroom wall above the headboard for many years. We came to see the dream as a visitation of our Third in the form of a pair of divine lovers.

Part 2

The Soul of Relationship:
Third Presence and
Sexual Communion

&

Four
Spiritual Chemistry and the Subtle Senses

Our subtle bodies know who we're becoming
Like a bee circling the bud it will enter later
Or the air feeling the wings of downy linnets
Before they learn to fly

We dreamt our spirit lovers
Appeared at the foot of the bed
Their transparent embrace inspiring
Us to match their closeness of being

How can we remember the bee, the wind
And our spirit lovers
In the middle of a busy day?

$\mathcal{T}$he erotic bonding needed to merge two personal myths is of a different nature from the familiar kind of sexual chemistry. Although strong physical attraction remains a welcomed ally, it is usually insufficient to fully illuminate a partnership story. Surrendering to the big picture of the relationship means going beyond projective love and even beyond the love inspired by the more conscious exchange of gifts.

The terrain is mysterious there. Our culture gives us little support for recognizing erotic attraction that is not based on visual images, imprinting from the families of origin, or a rational understanding of what the partners have to give each other. Yet the experience of this magnetism is not rare, as the following disclosures demonstrate.

"I'm drawn to her more all the time, but I can't tell you why. She's never really been my type and I've known women who had more to offer in concrete ways. But there's something about her—actually, about our *connection*—that's incredibly compelling. Sometimes when we're together I feel on the verge of seeing the world in a new light. My love for her is exciting and scary at the same time..."

"My husband and I have been married for almost twenty years. It's a miracle! There were so many times we almost came apart, like when the chemistry between us disappeared and we almost stopped making love...or when he realized he didn't want children and I had to give up having a family...or when I got so involved with meditation. Yet even when our differences seemed insurmountable, we knew we had to go on. However dark the problems, splitting up has always felt wrong. I don't know why, but our relationship and my spiritual life seem inseparable, even though we hardly ever meditate together. God only knows how our sexuality came to life again—and in a completely different and more subtle way..."

The chemistry of attraction in a long-term committed relationship has an evolving life of its own. Generally, the first major shift is away from image- projection and into an attraction based on the exchange of gifts. Then, around midlife or later, a new magnetism begins to develop that seems less connected to personalities, children, family, home, power in the world, or economic viability. While elusive and subtle at times, the new attraction is distinctly erotic but doesn't immediately or necessarily call for genital sexuality. The pull still involves the partner but also includes something larger that speaks of the partnership's innate wholeness and connection with spirit. We call this magnetism *spiritual chemistry*.

Spiritual chemistry is the yearning to be in touch with spirit through union with one's partner.

The image-projection form of chemistry that often ignites relationships has an autonomous nature more or less independent of the partners' behavior. Attraction arising from the exchange of gifts is largely based on establishing relationship patterns that increase the opportunities for mutual support. Spiritual chemistry has more to do with the *processes* of a relationship, particularly those that are empowered by honest communication. For a couple entering the transcending portion of their journey together, *honesty is the ultimate aphrodisiac.*

The activation of spiritual chemistry creates sustained and purposeful movement in the relationship that diminishes both partners' need to control what happens. Under the influence of spiritual chemistry, the relationship takes on a life—and voice—of its own. Neither partner is running the show. The relationship's direction and service to others seems to be shaped more and more by an unseen force.

Ultimately, letting go of control becomes a matter of trusting that "the relationship has your best interests in mind." The further you travel along the transcending path, doing the practices and the work of the relationship, the greater the trust, until you and your partner finally have no doubt that your process of individuation is well-served by the partnership.

The recognition of spiritual chemistry is seriously hindered by our culture's preoccupation with the more blatant attractions of secular sexuality. Many of us lament the latter's decline, as if that necessarily signifies that our relationships are in a terminal state. As a consequence, we frequently lack the insight or perseverance to discover what can follow the natural loss of secular chemistry. We lack models and a mythology of relationship that would help us prepare for an evolving sexuality in which spiritual chemistry plays an increasingly important role.

These deficiencies arise out of the fundamental polarization of Eros and Spirit in our cultural ethos. Typically, the separation between our sexual and spiritual lives starts in childhood as a reflection of family values and dynamics. For many of us, these early experiences transmit the message, either directly or indirectly, that sex and spirit are incompatible. We have found it productive to remember these seminal experiences and share them with each other. Jaquelyn's story is a dramatic example of a direct message.

I see my giant of a father, whom I adored, kneeling by his bedside each night and saying his prayers in childlike submission to Jesus. I can still hear him scolding me for calling him father. "I'm your dad!" he would say. "There's only one Father!" I have wonderful early images of him taking me fishing, walking with me in the woods, and reading to me from the Bible. Then around my eleventh birthday, about the time my breasts started budding and men began to look at me in a different way, he grew distant and less affectionate. The first time I wore lipstick he dragged me into the bathroom to scrub off my "war paint." "No daughter of mine is leaving this house looking like a whore!" he yelled. When he caught me smoking behind the barn with my brothers, he whipped me (but not the boys). "A girl who smokes would do *anything*," he said sternly. Of course, I was dying of curiosity to know what *anything* meant.

His religion began to sound harsh and restrictive to me. I felt a great loss when our fishing trips and walks came to an end. He took to shaking his head hopelessly when I acted boy crazy and said I was "going to the devil." I got the message. If I wanted to continue receiving my father's love—not to mention God's—I had to suppress the growing excitement and power I felt inside myself. I had to choose between being sexual and being spiritual. At the time, that wasn't a choice for me. When I refused to be baptized at the age of twelve, the gulf between us grew wider.

More often than not, any serious discomfort a father has with his daughter's developing erotic side tends to be repressed and so emerges indirectly. He might tell his nine-year-old cryptically that she is "too old" now to be sitting on Daddy's lap at story time. This kind of indirect message is more confusing to the daughter. She knows something is bothering daddy, but neither the issue nor her choices have been clearly illuminated.

Typically the analogous mother-son pattern also arises indirectly. Consider Jack's story.

I was a little plump as a teenager, in large part because my mother enjoyed providing our family with well-prepared, abundant meals. By the time high school was out in June and I left to take one of my strenuous summer jobs, I was at least fifteen pounds overweight. By early September the weight was gone and I returned to school slimmer and—I soon discovered—more attractive to my female classmates. My mother had a different reaction to my leanness. She thought I looked undernourished and promptly plied me with extra food. By Thanksgiving, the weight was back on and I got noticeably less attention from the girls.

Years later I realized that my mother had been disturbed (unconsciously, I'm quite sure) by the increase in my sexiness due to the loss of weight and promptly returned me to a condition that was more comfortable for her. I didn't understand what was happening either and, in any event, probably felt more at ease with the reduced level of attention.

My mother's indirect message was clear. Getting her full acceptance (and nourishment!) meant I had to limit my sexual presence. Since she largely carried the spiritual values in our family, I "learned" that my more robust sexual interests fell outside these values—and so a split was created.

Although the polarization of Eros and Spirit continues to play a major role in shaping our relationships, there are hopeful signs of movement in recent years. The gradual empowerment of women in our society has made them less willing to follow the longstanding cultural attitudes that separate spirituality from erotic relationship. The men's movement of the past twenty years has helped pry some males loose from their traditional attitudes about women, sex, and spirit. New opportunities exist now for a fundamental transformation in the way men and women relate.

The media's perspective on relationship also seems to be maturing a little. Despite the economically driven need to entertain, a few films have touched more realistically on relational themes, some in a lighthearted manner (for example, *When Harry Met Sally*). Although most of what appears on television and in films reinforces stereotypical sexual behavior, a few more daring productions have seriously questioned eroticism based only on secular chemistry. Change is also taking place through the spiritually-based, twelve-step codependency programs; an increasing number of books, conferences, and workshops that view relationship as a spiritual path; and revolutionary movements within traditional religious institutions that are devoted to healing the split between our erotic and spiritual lives (for example, Matthew Fox's "Creation Spirituality."[1])

---

[1] *Original Blessing: A Primer in Creation Spirituality*, Mathew Fox, Bear and Co.,1983.

&

An Awakening of Spiritual Chemistry

The progression from secular into spiritual chemistry is often tumultuous and painful, as the following example illustrates.

David learned as a young child not to trust others to take care of him. When he was still a teenager, he decided that his only safety lay in acquiring power and wealth. At the age of thirty-five, after he had already become a financially successful entrepreneur, he went searching for a wife to raise his son from a previous marriage and start a new family. David's list of requirements for a partner (which he had carefully written out!) included bearing and raising children, running the household, and frequent sex. Not having had much positive experience of it growing up, he relegated love to a place of secondary importance in creating his list of wifely duties.

Sarah seemed to be an excellent candidate for the "job." She was attractive, intelligent, a talented painter, mature enough to run a household efficiently, and with at least ten good childbearing years ahead of her. Although she had some resistance to the proposed arrangement, Sarah wanted children and, after living on the edge of poverty for many years, financial security meant a lot to her. David's business capabilities and resources were impressive, so she accepted his proposal. At that juncture, their sexual chemistry was decidedly secular, since it was empowered explicitly by their agreement and David's attraction to her beauty. After the wedding they moved into the mansion David had built on a bluff overlooking the Columbia River

Their first child was born ten months later and a second within another two years. Sarah was soon completely preoccupied with raising children and running their large household. She had little time for painting. David worked long hours, often returning home after the children were in bed. However, he did develop an interest in Christian mysticism, which he supported primarily by means of a voracious appetite for reading during the early hours of the morning. During these years, David made little connection between his spiritual exploration and his family life. He and Sarah had intercourse several times a week, usually accompanied by only a limited exchange of feeling. Sarah continued to see their sex life as her dutiful fulfillment of the original agreement.

Gradually Sarah became depressed and her health deteriorated. When her youngest child was three, she developed emphysema and nearly died. That led her to the realization that reconnecting with her art and building a strong inner life was essential for her survival. Being sexual with David became more difficult for her, but she couldn't risk telling him that directly. Although David wanted to continue making love as before, their waning secular chemistry no longer provided enough excitement to satisfy his needs. He felt that Sarah's lack of interest constituted a breech of their agreement. The absence of deep affection made intimacy increasingly difficult for both of them.

When they began therapy, both individually and conjointly, a separation was considered, but the children made that possibility unattractive. Therapeutic progress was slow until Sarah became more willing to be honest about her feelings and risk rocking the boat (by withholding sex more overtly, for example). David's ensuing anger, grief, and depression finally helped him recognize how foreign the "path of the heart" had always been to him. He saw that his much-desired spiritual awakening had more to do with loving Sarah than searching for God through the books he was reading. That insight radically changed his attitude about sex. He found himself less attracted to Sarah because of her physical appearance, but being intimate with her became increasingly magnetic in a way he didn't understand. At the same time, their unsatisfying sexual life reopened his youthful attraction to beautiful, sexy women. It was a time of great erotic confusion for David.

Simultaneously his entrepreneurial fortress started to crumble, exposing the tender and frightened side he had hidden since childhood. At first, his vulnerability made him more lovable to Sarah, particularly after he started reaching out to her for greater emotional support. Finally, sex became a source of some emotional nourishment for them both, as well as a way to release stress and for Sarah to fulfill her "obligations" to the marriage. David's stirrings of love and admiration for Sarah slowly found a voice, even as he grew more burdened with increasing business pressures.

As David's attraction to Sarah became part of his rocky path of the heart, he began to spend more time with her and the children. Feeling empowered by her individual therapy and David's growing involvement in the family, Sarah decided to return to school to study anthropology and ecology. The power balance in their relationship shifted, which helped to deepen their friendship. However, up to that point, Sarah's growing sense of spiritual awakening had little to do with her relationship with David, so it was left for him to search for a source of spiritual chemistry in their erotic life. He rose to the occasion. One day, about three years after they'd begun counseling, David acknowledged with tears in his eyes that his relationships with Sarah and the children had become the most important part of his life.

As David's business world fragmented further, he came to rely on Sarah for more and more of his sense of well-being. She tried to satisfy his neediness until it became a heavy burden for her on top of school and taking care of the children. When she challenged him to take care of his own emotional needs, their erotic life once again entered a turbulent phase.

Then their house began to slip down the bluff after a winter of heavy rains. Sarah got the message immediately, but it took David longer to see that he couldn't live in a fortress any longer, either physically or psychically. He realized finally that he had trans-ferred his lifelong "fortress mentality" from his house and business to his relationship with Sarah. It was time to trust in the direction his life was inexorably taking. He set the intention to stop using Sarah as his refuge and embraced the challenge to become self-accepting in a new way. That enabled David to envision turning over the reins of his business to others and using his considerable talents to do something that would "make my heart sing."

As David grew stronger, he began to see Sarah more objectively. He soon realized that her limited interest in their erotic life had less to do with him and more with her own deep fear of intimacy. He challenged her to include their erotic life in her growing sense of empowerment. Now it was Sarah's turn to look deeply into the dark mirror of relationship. After a session in which she broke down, acknowledged her fears, and spoke more honestly of her complex feelings for David, they embraced in our driveway for several minutes before driving off. Something had stirred in Sarah.

This brings their story to the present. If Sarah continues to use their relationship for self reflection, and if David can hold steadily to his path, then their newborn spiritual chemistry may well grow strong enough to draw them into a new cycle of mutual love and understanding.

8

Body Energy Fields

For the most part, secular sexual chemistry is celebrated through the five physical senses and experienced as magnetism between two physical and emotional bodies. In contrast, spiritual chemistry involves the *subtle senses* and magnetism between two *subtle bodies* or *energy fields*. To explore the mysteries of this kind of chemistry and its enhancement, we need to explore the nature of the energy field that interpenetrates our physical bodies. Learning to be aware of this field helps to develop our subtle senses, which in turn enhances all the primary practices of a transcending relationship.

The Seven Chakras

According to ancient mystery teachings from such traditions as Tantra, Kabala, and alchemy, an energy field surrounds and penetrates the human physical form, creating what is called the "etheric body." (Some occultists call this the "energetic double.") Briefly described in Chapter 1, the etheric body, which is not visible to most people, consists of an interweaving mesh of energy flows that link a set of anatomical centers with their etheric counterparts. There are seven primary etheric centers or *chakras* and innumerable secondary ones throughout the etheric body.

The chakras are focal points or concentrations of energy located primarily along a midline axis parallel to the spine and are related to certain endocrine glands. These centers are seen as intermediate linkages or channels that connect the physical and etheric bodies. The chakras can be detected by a simple process called *scanning*, which involves gentle passes of the hand around the body at a distance of a few inches. The energy of the centers is felt in the hand usually as some combination of tingling, change in temperature, and/or shift in density. Hand-scanning provides basic training for developing the subtle senses.

For simplicity, we will limit our attention to the seven major energy centers that have the greatest influence in shaping the subtle body. Gathering together various sources, the seven chakras can be described briefly as follows[2]:

1. *The root center* is located between the genitals and anus at the base of the spine and energetically connects us to the earth through our legs and feet, and also through our sense of smell. The root center is linked with the adrenal glands. It is the primary focus of our survival instinct and provides the energetic foundation for our health on the physical level. In particular, the root

---

[2] These include W. Brugh Joy, *Joy's Way*, J. P. Tarcher, 1978; C. Leadbeater, *The Chakras*, Theosophical Publishing House, 1972; Rudolf Steiner, *Knowledge of the Higher Worlds and Its Attainment*, Anthroposophic Press, 1947; and our own experiences exploring energy fields through hand-scanning.

center is associated with the skeletal, peripheral vascular, lymph, and nervous systems.

2. *The sexual or reproductive center* is located in women a short distance beyond the deepest point in the vagina, midway between the ovaries, and in men just behind and slightly below the prostate gland. This chakra is linked with our procreative capacity and the physical nature of our sexuality. Our eroticism is literally grounded here. The sexual center also influences our sense of taste and is related to the ovaries and testicles, along with all their hormones.

3. *The solar plexus center* is located just above the umbilicus and mediates our sense of identity in the world—our "place in the sun." The status of the solar plexus center characterizes our emotional connections to people, power, work, money, and other major cultural elements. In short, it is the seat of our worldly or secular personality. This emotional center is also associated with nutritional assimilation and the pancreas.

4. *The heart center* is located under the sternum along the midline of the chest and is linked with our sense of touch and capacity for compassion towards self and others. Awareness that all forms of life are interconnected is associated with the activated heart center, which is the seat of our desire to provide service to others. An activated heart chakra brings awareness that we are all in this mystery called life *together* and that anything that harms one ultimately harms all. The heart is connected with the thymus gland (which plays a central role in the immune system).

5. *The throat center* is located near the larynx and is connected with the thyroid gland. The throat chakra is related to our sense of hearing and our faculties of creative and artistic expression. The throat is the seat of our intuition and acts as a connection between the capacity for thought (located at the brow chakra) and the first four centers.

In scanning body fields, it is often noted that the throat and sexual centers have an inverse relationship: when an individual has an extremely active sexual center, often the throat will be "quieter," and vice versa. This unusual pattern has been the subject of much debate. Many have concluded that the throat cannot really open unless the sexual center is significantly restrained and its energy redirected. For example, Alice Bailey wrote[3]:

> When the energies of the sacral [sexual] centre, focused hitherto on the work of physical creation and generation and therefore the source of physical sex life and interest, are sublimated, re-oriented and carried up to the throat centre, then the aspirant becomes a conscious creative force in the higher worlds; he enters within the veil, and begins to create the pattern of things which will bring about eventually the new heavens and the new earth.

The need to redirect sexual energy in order to fully realize oneself in these "higher worlds" provides the anatomical foundation for the ascetic (or celibate) path of spiritual awakening. We agree that unconscious expression of the procreative urge and habitual sexual patterns (attachment to orgasmic discharge during intercourse, for example) are not consistent with an open throat center. A variety of nonsexual alternatives for expressing erotic energy do need to be available if one is to develop strong intuitive and creative faculties.

However, we envision this being accomplished not by restraining or closing down the sexual center but by *transcending the inverse energy pattern itself*. It is our conviction that the sexual and throat centers can—indeed, must—be open simultaneously in both partners for relationship to flower erotically, creatively, and spiritually.

6. *The brow center or "third eye"* is located in the middle of the forehead, just above the eyes, and is considered the seat of self-awareness. Related to the pituitary gland, this center is the source

[3]*A Treatise on White Magic or The Way of the Disciple*, Alice Bailey, Lucas Publishing Co., 1951, p. 192.

of our ability to be conscious that we are conscious (to whatever degree we have achieved that state); it houses our capacity for thought, image-making, and the use of symbols to convey ideas and feelings. When strongly activated, the brow center promotes development of clairvoyance and other psychic abilities.

7. *The crown center* is located just above the top of the head and is sometimes called the "thousand petaled lotus." Connected to the pineal gland, it is the seat of the most subtle or refined energy in our consciousness and the threshold to nonphysically-based states of awareness. In many religions the crown center is considered to be the locus of mystical experience, visions, and revelations. In Christian art, for example, it is often portrayed as a halo above the head of a saint or other holy person. It is said that at the crown level, time as we know it in ordinary reality does not exist; there is only the present. The nature of duality is transcended in crown consciousness and the physical and nonphysical worlds are no longer polarized in this state.

In addition to its value in probing the mysteries of intimate relationship, the chakral system has also been useful in our therapeutic work as a psycho-spiritual map of the human condition. Once one becomes familiar with the energy centers, it is no longer necessary to formally scan a person to perceive the activity level of each chakra and the overall state of the etheric field. What does seem necessary to sensing the subtle body with accuracy is the creation of a feeling rapport with the person, whether it be through attentive conversation or a few minutes of meditation together before the session starts. The interaction of the etheric fields of client and therapist in open sensitive communication elicits an intuitive knowing that transcends the ordinary mind. This happens to even a greater degree between two compatible lovers, whether a chakral map is being used consciously or not.

The usefulness of the chakral system in healing, therapeutic, and relational settings is not surprising. If you can assess someone's physical status...sexuality...emotional, relational, and work life...ability to love and desire to serve others...creative expression and intuitive capability...mental capacity and self-awareness...and spiritual consciousness—you have a good jump on describing the whole person!

Dyadic Energy Exercises

When two people are in close proximity to each other, their subtle bodies interact in a complex way. The subtle sensations each person experiences in response to sensing the partner's etheric field can run the gamut from repulsion to attraction, with an endless variety of reactions in-between. The response depends on the person's sensitivity to energy and the compatibility of the two fields. Responses also vary from moment to moment, depending on both people's moods, physical health, attentiveness, and so on. However, between two people who are intimately related, there is usually a core or "steady-state component" of the response that remains present more or less independently of the many changes that take place over time.

The spiritual chemistry between two people is the steady-state magnetic quality in the interaction of their subtle bodies.

Can spiritual chemistry be measured? Various forms of meditation alter the subtle body in different ways and offer a means of refining one's ability to use the subtle senses. Similarly, specific energy interaction exercises can help couples become more familiar with sensing the intermingling of their subtle bodies. Since spiritual chemistry depends on the strength of the magnetism in this intermingling, energy interaction practices permit direct perception of a couple's spiritual chemistry—and, at the same time, provide the opportunity to enhance it.

Enhancement comes about because of the "laws" that govern energy fields and, therefore, influence spiritual chemistry. Once a certain critical level of magnetism and sensitivity has been reached, the nature of spiritual chemistry is such that, in due time, its direct perception will increase the magnetism and each partner's sensitivity to it, *if that is the couple's intention.*[4] In other words, *the practice of becoming more aware of subtle body interactions gives lovers the opportunity to increase their sexual chemistry.*

Encountering non-ordinary reality with an intimate partner is a different experience from entering subtle states of consciousness alone. For many people, visionary experiences are more accessible when they are stimulated by intimate dyadic practices. The presence of a partner holding a similar intention helps to verify, expand, and refine an individual's perceptions of the Imaginal Realm. The commitment to report to each other afterwards stimulates both partners' ability to describe the visionary landscape they have explored together.

We will limit our attention here to a few practices that expand awareness of subtle body interactions. The imaginative couple will have no difficulty in creating a wide variety of similar exercises that suit their particular tastes and situations. Except when an alternative is specifically mentioned, these practices are to be done sitting upright in a cross-legged position, using back rests or chairs as needed. Comfort is essential. Generally, the back should be as vertical as possible, with the spine straight and legs and arms positioned to avoid tension. In most dyadic meditations the eyes remain open, either focused or slightly unfocused, depending on the intention of the particular practice.

Hand-scanning. Scanning each other's energy field using simple hand passes allows the partners to explore each other's subtle body directly and is an excellent first step in developing energy interaction practices. The partner being scanned lies flat on his or her back, preferably on a massage table or high bed, so that the scanner can stand comfortably and avoid strain. The scanning partner

---

[4] These laws are analogous to those of quantum physics. In particular, we refer here to the Heisenberg principle which implies, simplistically speaking, that nothing can be measured without changing it. Analogously, when two people become conscious of their spiritual chemistry, the magnetism between them changes and will increase with time if that is their "loving intention."

relaxes and centers her- or himself by means of attentive breathing or other meditative techniques. With arm and hand extended, palm down, the scanner then moves through the etheric field, a few inches from the partner's body, making gentle sweeps and passes. The prone partner also moves into a meditative state, keeping the mind open and releasing expectations.

The scanner explores the entire field, paying particular attention to the seven main centers. At first very little may be felt. That is of no significance, because energy interaction is occurring whether perceived or not. As the scanner becomes quieter and moves further into a meditative state, awareness of the partner's subtle body may increase. Disbelief, self-judgment ("Am I doing this right?"), and many other disruptive thoughts may also arise. Let them go gently. Eventually, perception begins to develop not only through the sensations in the hand but also via associated images and thoughts that enter the mind spontaneously. With practice, scanning becomes a readily accessible way to enter and explore the Imaginal Realm with one's partner.

Chakral journey. Facing each other in the basic sitting position, partners "warm up" with a little synchronized deep breathing. Slowly they set the intention to bring their awareness to the interaction of their subtle bodies. After a few moments one of the partners, acting as the verbal guide, invites them both to begin a journey of exploration and attunement, starting at the root center. The other partner becomes the guide at the sexual center, and they continue alternating as guides until they reach the crown. At each step, the guide suggests that they both bring their attention first to their own center, then to their partner's, and finally to the connection between the two. The guide describes the universal attributes associated with each center in an inviting voice, using whatever words and images arise spontaneously. Recall:

root center: health and vitality

pelvic center: sexuality and procreation

solar plexus center: emotions, personal power, and identity

heart center: love and the interconnectedness of all life

throat center: creativity and intuition

brow center: the mystery of the mind and self-awareness

crown center: spiritual presence and wholeness

The journey's pace is slow, relaxed, and exploratory. The intention is to sense the field, not to judge or evaluate. The practice allows etheric energy to flow openly between the partner's centers, helping them move towards a natural balancing of their subtle bodies. The experience is often both erotic (since it increases spiritual chemistry) and healing. In addition, partners become more accepting of the existence of their joint field—that is, the third field created as a result of the intermingling of their two subtle bodies. This "dance of the fields" often initiates awareness of Third Presence.

At first, such experiences of Third Presence are fleeting and may be difficult to retain after the exercise. But if energy interaction practices become a regular part of the partners' relationship, awareness of the Third lingers with prolonged interpenetration of their subtle bodies. When used in conjunction with dyadic council, scanning and chakral journeys are a great asset in harmonizing personality differences as well as expanding contact with the Third.

"Breathlight." This meditation, which is excellent for energizing the subtle body, can be done alone or with a partner as a preparation for other dyadic practices. Assuming the basic sitting position with eyes closed or open, begin by relaxing and quieting the body with several long, slow breaths. Now start the meditation.

On the inhale, imagine that you are pulling your breath up from the center of the earth through the bottom of your feet and into your sexual energy center. If you like to visualize in color, imagine this breath from the earth to be a deep vibrant red. Then with the exhale let the rich, red, earth-sexual breath radiate out from your sexual center into every cell of your body, invigorating and enlivening all your organs and tissues.

Alternate the inbreath from the earth with one that emanates from a bright white light a foot or two above your head. Bring the light down by inhaling it through your entire upper body, coming to rest at the end of inhalation in the sexual center. Now exhale this light-sexual breath outward from the sexual center to all the cells of your body, as you did with the earth-sexual breath, enlightening every part of your being.

Continue breathing in and out of your sexual center, slowly letting all your attention focus there. Imagine it being energized, first by the red breath of the earth and then by the white breath of spirit. Imagine these two breaths are in an interpenetrating dance. Allow them to enter the sexual center slowly, as if they were going to make love with each other. Then with the exhale, send this sexual love out to every part of your body.

In your mind's eye, see the sexual center as the point of connection between the heavens above and the earth below. Imagine you are breathing in earth and light and sending out sexual love to every cell of your body. Continue, staying aware of the level of energy in your sexual center. You may feel a subtle erotic charge that starts in the genital area and then extends throughout the whole body. Stay with the energy; be present with the feelings for a while without suppressing them or discharging them through familiar sexual fantasies or activity.

Eye resonance. This exercise is an adaptation of a Gurdjieffian (originally Tibetan) technique that helps increase subtle body interaction between partners—often dramatically. The practice, which is suitable for a single couple or groups of couples, is simple but profound. The partners sit in the basic sitting position, facing each other, without touching. Each partner looks steadily into the other's left eye, trying not to blink or look away. This interpenetrating stare is held for at least ten minutes—*silently*. The time may seem to pass very slowly.

If desired, partners can then take turns sharing what they've experienced. Sometimes this exercise creates a surplus of energy that may manifest through laughter or crying. A small amount of tearing is common. Facial images often change dramatically, taking on strange human or animal-like forms. It is not unusual during eye resonance to feel transported to a time in the distant past or forward into the future.

Eye resonance is particularly useful for people who feel they have a limited capability for imaging. Workshop participants sometimes report that this exercise provided their first experience of spontaneous visionary imaging with their eyes wide open. Eye resonance is an excellent preparation for observing spontaneous images that arise from any practice that stimulates non-ordinary states of consciousness.

Slow talking. This unusual form of dyadic council is especially effective for highly verbal people and those who live "in their heads" a lot of the time. With their eyes wide open, partners face each other in basic sitting position and take a few slow, relaxing breaths. They then begin a regular dyadic council except that each person speaks v - e - r - - - y - - - - s - l - o - w - - - l - y - - - - w - i - t - h - - - - p - a - u - s - - - e - s - - - - b - e - - - t - w - e - e - n - - - - e - v - - - e - r - - - y syllable and word. Obviously the theme for this kind of council needs to be one that lends itself to making brief statements. In our workshops we usually ask each couple to exchange a few short vows that arise spontaneously from the current state of their relationship. The vows can involve commit-ments to activities or attitudes that will help move the relation-ship further along the transcending path.

"I vow to show up at our regular weekly councils, ready to honestly share my thoughts and feelings."

"I vow to make time for playing and hanging out together."

"I vow to be slow and artful in our lovemaking and not just plunge into genital contact."

The listener has to pay close attention to his or her partner in order to understand what is being said. S-l-o-w speaking brings about s-l-o-w thinking, which usually moves both partners into a more perceptive and attentive state of consciousness. In general, slowing down is conducive to the perception of non- ordinary reality. This exercise reveals, often with much humor, how the speed at which we habitually talk and think can block subtle awareness. The reader might reread this section very slowly now to observe the trance-like effect s-l-o-w talking has on the mind and body.

Embrace meditation. As a regular practice, the embrace medita-tion stimulates erotic energy, eases tension, and provides a good alternative to lovemaking for couples who have been sexually inactive for one reason or another (for example, after childbirth). The embrace meditation offers an effective way for the couple to reawaken physical intimacy gently, without any pressure to be genitally active.

Generally a good time of day to do the meditation is early in the morning in bed just after awakening, perhaps right after sharing dreams, when partners are rested and before the day's activities begin. Some couples with young children prefer a time late in the evening when the household has finally settled down. We recommend about twenty minutes be devoted to the medita-tion, which can be extended if time permits and inclination supports.

To describe the exercise, we assume the larger partner is the man. Whoever is larger lies on "his" back, legs extended and uncrossed. The smaller person lies next to him on "her" side to his left, her left leg thrown over his thighs and her left arm extended across his chest. Her weight is almost entirely supported by the bed, not by her partner. A pillow under her head may help. The woman's other arm and leg can be placed in any comfortable position. The man embraces his partner with the arm that is closest to her and finds a comfortable position for his other hand—for example, on her thigh, shoulder, or head. It is important to be completely comfortable, without any feeling of heaviness or strain. In this position the partners' hearts are near each other and their genitals are close but not necessarily touching. No words are exchanged. Breathing is slow and gentle.

Inhale gently through the nose and let your exhale pass through the boundaries between your two bodies (the thighs and the chest, for example). After a while these boundaries may seem to dissolve, until finally the feeling is of one body breathing. Listen to your own heartbeat and then the heartbeat of your partner. Embrace both as parts of a unified single rhythm. Let the mind slowly become still as you become filled with the sweetness of the silence. The eyes can be open, closed, or resting unfocused on your partner or on some object in the room. The intention is to remain this side of sleep. If you find yourself drifting off, open your eyes...

If you feel genital stirring and/or a desire to make love, slow the breathing down and use your exhaling to guide the erotic energy in the pelvic area upward and downward into the chest and legs. Be still. Let your arousal bring awareness of the vessel the two of you are creating. Gently move away from critical and evaluative thinking...

As the meditation ends, stir and disengage slowly. Give yourself a few moments before you arise. You may like to remain in the afterglow of the meditation for several minutes.

When making love is in the offing, the embrace meditation can provide a gentle transition from the stresses of daily life. Some couples do the meditation in the evening just before sleep as a calming way to end the day and encourage dreamsharing. A few couples have found it possible to continue the meditation even when interrupted by young children and so are able to share a part of their intimate life appropriately with the rest of the family.

Many couples will recognize this exercise as an elaboration of a familiar "cuddling" position—which brings up an important point. Many of the practices we have found effective in cultivating spiritual chemistry and Third Presence are simple, non-esoteric, and even familiar. What is important is the *intention* and the *attention* the couple bring to the activity. In the case of the embrace meditation, the intention is to heighten awareness of the interaction of subtle bodies and so stimulate receptivity to the Third. During the meditation partners are attentive to the breath, patterns of thought, body sensations, and the interplay of subtle bodies.

Although the general intentions in doing the practice may be clear, it is also important to release specific expectations each time it is performed in order to let the process unfold spontaneously. As partners embrace each other, they also embrace undirected or "leisure mind," which invites the unpredictable to enter.

Five
Invoking Third Presence

The first time for you was at the Inn
When you were touched by something larger
Than two bodies making love
For me it happened kneeling in front of your chair
In the living-room a year later on a Sunday

Our eyes were making love when a door opened
I didn't even know existed
And for a suspended moment my mind
Let go its hold while I breathed
The sweet air of freedom

A year after we started doing the embrace meditation regularly, we had our first prolonged experience of Third Presence. Jaquelyn's journal entry for that day describes the spontaneous event.

We rolled sleepily into each other's arms about five in the morning. We had intended to make love the night before, but exhaustion claimed us first and we had fallen into a deep sleep. We slipped easily into the embrace meditation, dozing now and then. After about half an hour, I became conscious of how sweet and delicious Jack's body was and how perfectly we fit together. The obvious evidence of his arousal prompted me to ask jokingly whom he had been dreaming about. "You, of course," he said with a sly smile and we lapsed again into the trance-like state that had now become familiar. Our breathing became imperceptible, like whisper-breaths in the early morning stillness.

Then I gradually became aware of a presence that felt like a subtle, porous, spongy comforter barely touching us. The stiller we became, the stronger the presence felt. When at times it seemed to enter as well as surround us, I would drift into a state of oblivion for a few moments. I began to lose sense of the boundaries of our bodies, until it felt like we were a single being, although, paradoxically, I still retained "I- consciousness" and assumed Jack did as well. Then slowly I became aware of a distinct presence that included both of us but also had its own tangible identity.

At first I held my breath, trying to suspend time and hold onto the intense sweetness I felt. When I began to relax and breathe again, I realized that the presence was always there, although my awareness of it shifted with my breathing. I wondered if we had found the "etheric earth" that Rudolf Steiner wrote about.[1] Wherever we were, we definitely had expanded beyond the boundaries of our physical bodies and entered a world of subtle matter.

This delightful state lasted for several minutes, during which I saw clearly (the perception had nothing to do with regular vision or my ordinary mind) that a "third con-

---

[1] *The True Nature of the Second Coming*, Rudolf Steiner, Anthroposophical Publishing Co., 1961.

sciousness" existed in our relationship beyond the limitations of our personalities. A feeling of presence in this state was palpable but not of the ordinary world. The state was so real that I wanted to name it...

In the months that followed we encountered this presence on several occasions: in council, when we meditated together, but most often during lovemaking. We found that our awareness of it increased when we were open, honest, and non-defensive with each other. The most important factors in sensing the presence, however, were a heightening of our spiritual chemistry and an increase in the vitality of our imaginative interactions. Sometimes, when we were delighting in planning a workshop or talking about the mysteries of our relationship, we would realize suddenly that we were not alone.

In this third presence we saw the truth of whatever we were talking about more directly and clearly. The experience was not that of deducing the insight ourselves but of having it revealed by a gifted teacher. We came to see these incidents as revelatory gifts from the Imaginal Realm. In the context of traditional shamanism, for example, we saw that encountering this third consciousness was similar to receiving insight from one's power animal or spirit guide during a shamanic journey.

Finally, we decided to honor our ongoing experience by identifying third consciousness as the presence of an otherworldly ally. We started calling this expanded state of awareness *Third Presence* and allowed ourselves to talk about the source of insight affectionately as "the Third." The association of a spirited synergistic third presence with a loving relationship is not new. As our Third became a more familiar companion over a period of several years, we discovered others had encountered a similar state of awareness.[2]

---

[2] See, for example, Robert Bly in his fine poem, "A Third Body," from the collection *Loving a Woman in Two Worlds*, Harper & Row, 1985; *Divine Madness*, John R. Haule, Shambhala, 1990; and *Fire in the Heart: Everyday Life as Spiritual Practice*, Roger Hosden, Element Books, 1990.

It became clear to us that Third Presence was a distinctive state of awareness associated with the transcendent dimension of our relationship. For Jaquelyn the awareness was often associated with a specific movement of energy between her sexual and heart centers. For Jack, the energy field around the head and heart seemed expanded and more luminous when the Third was about. In Third Presence both of us felt we had entered a joint state of non-ordinary consciousness in which we were able to see, hear, and feel with heightened intuitive perception.

We anticipated that seeing the Third as a *functional entity* would also help couples we worked with to make contact with the transcendent aspects of their relationship in a more tangible and personal way. We also knew that skepticism would arise. Laurence LeShan thoroughly explores the existence of such functional constructs and concludes that asking a question such as, "Does the Third really exist?" is ultimately irrelevant.[3] The important issue concerning functional entities—in contrast with what he calls "structural entities" (for example, material objects)—is not whether they exist but *whether their use is beneficial.* This has indeed been the case with the Third. The notion of Third Presence and the practices that stimulate entry into this state of awareness have been quite useful to us and many other couples, now over a period of many years.

The basic challenge in identifying the transcending qualities of relationship with a construct called Third Presence is to remind ourselves regularly that we are really talking about an expanded state of consciousness that is *co-created by two partners together with something unconditional and ultimately mysterious that is not of the ordinary world.* This means that exploration of the Third will never be "complete." Every couple who enters the Third Presence will continue to make new discoveries about the nature of this state of consciousness.

---

[3] *Alternate Realities: The Search for the Full Human Being,* Laurence LeShan, Ballantine, 1976.

As our exploration continued, we discovered that encounters with the Third are often associated with *breaks in the pattern of ordinary reality* that, at different times, are joyous, enlightening, painful, frightening, or disorienting. We also found that entering Third Presence required that partners let go of trying to control each other and the relationship. Spontaneous encounters with Third Presence typically fell into one of four broad categories.

- *A time of intense sexual interaction in which a new level of communion is experienced.* This may occur in the ecstatic state just before orgasm, especially when the couple delay climax and instead "ride the wave" to a new level of erotic awareness. When partners are preoccupied with performance, control, or other personality level issues during lovemaking, however, the Third is far less likely to "show up."

- *A time of peak co-creativity* (artistic, athletic, or spiritual, for example), particularly during a period when the depth of collaboration has moved to a new level. Usually these situations require that both partners be deeply involved in the activity; often they occur after an interval of intense focus. Examples include a prolonged hike into beautiful and challenging terrain, a long period of dyadic meditation (for example, during a several-day silent retreat), or collaborating on a piece of writing—such as a book on relationship!

- *A time of grief, fear, or sudden adversity.* We often become aware of the profundity of our relationships when we most fear their loss. A crisis, particularly if it involves a threat to health, often radically shifts priorities and awakens partners to Third Presence.

- *Sensing the perfection of creation while being together in nature.* Humility and childlike wonder create a fertile environment for the Third to make its appearance.

(Recall Jesus' teaching [paraphrasing]: "Come unto me as a child."[4])

The Nature of Third Presence

We find that Third Presence invariably fills us with a sense of "coming home," despite the sometimes brutal candor of the insights we receive. The kind of love encountered in this state is often "tough" and never sentimental. Yet we are rarely defensive in encounters with the Third, even though we are so deeply seen in its presence. The familiar pattern of protecting the other—and, of course, at the same time ourselves—from shadowy thoughts and feelings dissipates in Third Presence. When the Third is around us (literally!), the complexities of our interactions are more readily untangled and the relationship feels simpler. We are repeatedly shown that the greatest tension in our relationship is created by avoiding the truth of what's actually happening between us.

The Archetype of the Divine Pair

Normally most people function as if they were separate beings of finite dimension living inside the boundary of their skins. This is particularly true in worldly life but only relatively less so in intimate partnership. In our early explorations of Third Presence, however, particularly in moments of erotic intensity, we found ourselves remarkably aware of our subtle bodies and how they interacted with each other. The illusion of being a separate entity faded. Instead, each of us felt immersed in the field that extends beyond our physical bodies, includes the other, and also *a knowing presence having an origin outside our joint field.*

This source of knowingness opened our hearts and induced a feeling of peace. We recognized that we were in a state of grace.

---

[4] Luke 18:16-17, *Holy Bible*, King James Version.

The intermingling of our subtle bodies became a celebration of the "mystery of two becoming one."[5]

We associated this mysterious quality of the Third with a gentle influx of relational energy encountered in the Imaginal Realm. The source was accessible only when we were feeling exceptionally relaxed and close to each other. Our ability to detect this refined presence was more likely in a state that combined meditation, passionate eroticism, and, most importantly, a heightened level of creative imagination.

Gradually, we grew to sense this influx of energy as a dual spirit or embodiment of relationship we called the "Divine Pair" or "Divine Lovers."[6] We thought of the Divine Pair as an archetype of the Imaginal Realm, in the early stages of being recognized, that would eventually embody a collective image of relationship beyond ordinary form and thought.

Once again we allowed ourselves to relate our personal experience to a *functional entity*, trusting that the identification would prove useful as long as we remained clear about the ultimately indescribable nature of what we were naming. There are, of course, many mythological lovers in our collective human history— Isis and Osiris, Shiva and Sakti, Zeus and Hera—to name just a few. However, the Divine Pair seemed transcultural to us, more like the common essence of all these mythological couples.

The Soul of the Relationship

In a single sentence then, *the Third is a unique functional entity—the soul of the relationship—created by the interpenetration of the partners' subtle bodies together with emanations of the Divine Pair.*[7]

---

[5] The first time we heard this compelling phrase was in a talk given by Joseph Campbell at The Ojai Foundation in 1982.

[6] It was interesting for us to reread William Irwin Thompson's *The Time Falling Bodies Take To Light: Mythology, Sexuality and the Origins of Culture*, St. Martin's Press, 1981, and discover that at the close of the book he shares the vision that the "avatars of the New Age" will not be the solitary male but the male and the female together.

[7] It is sufficient for our present purposes to use the word *soul* in its familiar poetic meaning as the deepest essence of the human condition. For a more extensive discussion of soul and the Imaginal Realm, see Appendix 1.

As a "personal" link to the Imaginal Realm, the Third helps its human partners become aware of their capacity to love in a way that is ideally and uniquely theirs. The partners feel the Third's touch in dreams and life experiences as a guiding intelligence that creates exactly what is needed to move their relationship along the transcending path. During lovemaking and other times of heightened communion, Third Presence expands with the intermingling of the partners' subtle bodies. At such moments, the grace of the Divine Pair becomes more available. In brief, each Third uniquely connects the ordinary and transcendent aspects of the relationship that it is serving.

❥

The Birth and Care of an Abiding Third

Recognizing the Third's existence is like a later-in-life version of birthing a child. Physical birth combines many aspects of the parents (and their ancestors), together with a mysterious component that is uniquely the child's. Analogously, the Third can be seen as a manifestation of the couple's Divine Child, who incorporates the subtle bodies of both partners and who (like most incarnate children) becomes a strong teacher and reflector of truth.[8]

We believe the potential for realizing Third Presence is inherent in the human capacity for relating. This potential remains latent until the moment of a relationship's "spiritual birth" when the commitment to the transcendent path is actually made. Needless to say, the spiritual birth (if it occurs at all) can take place before, during, or considerably after a formal marriage ceremony.

After its awakening, each Third's evolution depends on the strength of the partners' intention, their perseverance, and their skill in creating a fruitful environment for its development. Committing to a set of relational practices and carrying them out with

---

[8] The divine child archetype appears universally in history and mythology, the most familiar manifestation in Western culture being the Christ Child.

imagination and devotion are primary in establishing such an environment.

Once the relationship begins its path of transcendence, the Third takes on a life of its own. The genie doesn't go back in the bottle—at least, not without a struggle. The Third is a staunch and persistent ally of the relationship in its continued evolution. As the partners learn to listen and be guided, they move organically through the stages of their journey, spurred on by the power of their erotic connection and imaginative capabilities. At each stage, there are early glimpses of what is to come, then more abundant revelations, and finally the concrete challenges involved in manifesting the expanding vision authentically in their practices and life patterns.

Visionary Imagination

Dyadic council, energy interactions, dreamsharing, and a creative sexual life are the primary practices we have used to nourish the Third's development. All of these ultimately involve the expansion of ordinary imaginative capability to the visionary level. *Visionary imagination* is essential to the exploration of Third Presence.

The great Renaissance physician Paracelsus believed that imagination was the most creative force in humans because it has the power to call into existence varying forms of the soul. The nontraditional Islamic Sufis of the twelfth and thirteenth centuries (such as Rumi and Ibn 'Arabi) maintained that the mechanism of visionary imagination, or what they called creative imagination, provided a meeting place within the psyche for communion with the gods.[9] Islam, Buddhism, and Christianity are based on the spiritual visions, dreams, and "angelic" visitations of their founders and disciples.[10]

---

[9] See *Creative Imagination in the Sufism of Ibn 'Arabi*, and *Spiritual Body and Celestial Earth*, Henry Corbin, Princeton University Press, 1969 and 1977, respectively.
[10] For example, see *The Varieties of Religious Experience*, William James, Random House Modern Library Edition, 1936, p. 471; and the *Holy Bible*, King James Version, Acts:3-6.

Visionary imagination is our primary bridge to the Imaginal Realm. It allows us to learn the language of this level of consciousness and "bring back" teachings to inspire our daily lives. To a great extent, our capacity for visionary imagination determines the ecstatic and revelatory nature of both our erotic and spiritual lives. Erotic passion and visionary imagination are allies—in fact, inseparable partners—in helping us awaken to the Mystery. *Developing visionary imagination in the context of intimate relationship produces the sense-impressions, images, and awareness that are the lifeblood of Third Presence.*

In addition, the relational context allows visionary imagination to be readily integrated into ordinary life. Every spiritual path and vision of divinity is ultimately concerned with the ability to love *self* and *other*. In the spiritually awakening environment of a transcending relationship the many practices of erotic love provide a direct opportunity for developing this ability.[11]

Visionary imagination differs significantly from the other familiar kinds of imaginative activity. In *ordinary daydreaming or fantasy*, we usually mix remembrances of the past with the visual creation of future events that fulfill our desires, allay our fears, or satisfy some other emotional need. Most sexual fantasies fall into this category. *Directed fantasy* also occurs naturally when individuals prepare for some future event or action by mentally rehearsing. The fantasies passively induced by the voice in *hypnosis* or *guided meditation* are other instances of this kind of imaginative activity.

Since fantasies are often motivated by feelings of either desire or fear, they are akin to the familiar wish-fulfillment and anxiety-reducing functions of dreams. Both fantasizing and this kind of compensatory dreaming are personal and individualistic. But we

---

[11] Even though they are usually experienced as part of one's interior life, the images and insights reached through visionary imagination can feel as authentic as ordinary reality— even more so as one becomes accustomed to exploring the Imaginal Realm. As a result, many of us speak of these experiences as if they existed separately and distinctly in geographic "places," "planes," or "levels." Such figures of speech should not be taken literally. We always need to remember that the Imaginal Realm is basically an expanded state of consciousness that arises through interaction with the Mystery.

also have dreams that contain symbols and figures representing transpersonal elements of the psyche shared across the span of time and culture. Jung hypothesized that these elemental psychic instincts or archetypes arise from a *collective unconscious*, created out of the accumulated experiences of humankind, that is transpersonal and transcultural in nature.[12]

Besides appearing in dreams, *monadic archetypes* (for example, the wise old man and woman, the sorcerer and sorceress, the fool, and the king and queen) manifest in myths, fairy tales, and virtually every mystical tradition. How we participate in the creation of myths and dreams of an archetypal nature resembles the process of visionary imagination, except, of course, the latter can take place also when the conscious mind is awake and in a heightened state.

Active imagination is another more intentional image-creating process, also developed by Jung.[13] In this process one selects a particular image or figure (often one that first appeared in a dream) and, after a period of deep relaxation, encourages a sequence of visionary images and events to unfold. The imaginer, functioning primarily as a witness (and sometimes with the assistance of a guide or therapist), releases mental control, allowing a story to emerge that soon takes on a life of its own.

In an analogous way, we can define *visionary imagination as the capacity to make meaning out of spontaneous events—images, feelings, and thoughts—that connect our psychic and physical worlds.* Typically, such events are associated with...

- artistic inspiration, prayer, meditation, and other contemplative practices; or

- heightened personal interactions and sudden intrusions on our well-being that challenge the illusion of personal control.

[12] *The Archetypes and the Collective Unconscious, Vol. 9(1), The Collected Works of C.G. Jung*, Bollingen Series XX, Princeton University Press, 1959.
[13] See *Encounters with the Soul: Active Imagination as Developed by C.G. Jung*, Barbara Hanna, Sigo Press, 1981.

Visionary imagination thrives when personal will is surrendered to the sovereignty of the process. This surrender is motivated either consciously or unconsciously by our innate yearning for contact with the divine. Mystics have long believed that human consciousness and the Mystery interact and evolve through the process of visionary imagination. One might say that visionary imagination is the "language" that links human and divine consciousness. For a couple on the path of transcending relationship, a primary part of this link is provided by the *dyadic archetype* of the Divine Pair. The Divine Pair conveys its particular manifestation of the Mystery through the medium of Third Presence.

There is also a shadow side to visionary imagination. Traditional shamanism and countless mystics have spoken of the many dangers along the visionary path—dangers the rest of us usually discover the hard way! The Imaginal Realm is home to both diabolical and angelic images; Christ and Satan both reside in our collective imaginal consciousness. The archetypes of the Imaginal Realm can both guide and possess us. It is possible to become obsessed or lost learning to negotiate the terrain.[14]

The co-creative use of visionary imagination can also lead to entrapment by shadow images. The major challenge is to guard against partners falling into a joint inflation. A relationship can become a "two- person cult," in which the couple get carried away with a joint vision and become isolated from the reflection of others.

However, an open, honest, and confrontative relationship tends to be self-correcting and offers "built-in" protection against entrapment by shadow patterns. In a relatively conscious relationship, one partner can "mind the store" if the other should get lost in the Imaginal Realm. Dyadic councils witnessed by a friend or another couple, and setting aside time to listen silently to the Third are ways to guard against the pitfalls of partners getting lost together.

---

[14] The shadow side of the visionary path is discussed further in Appendix 1.

Visionary Imagination Practices

A particularly good way to stimulate co-creative visionary imagination is through what we call *mutual guided imagery*. In this practice, partners sit facing each other in comfortable meditative positions, close but not touching, eyes unfocused or closed. A theme for a visionary journey, event, or interaction is agreed upon beforehand. Then, after a few moments of relaxed breathing, one partner begins to set the scene in a languid, clear voice. After a bit, the other partner picks up the thread of the story and continues. They weave back and forth, holding the intention of being present in the world they are co-creating, all their physical and subtle senses awakened and receptive. The process proceeds spontaneously until a natural completion is felt and the partners acknowledge closure of their co-visioning experience together. Themes for this process include:

- an elaborate ritual of lovemaking in some exotic setting;

- a journey over (or under) the sea to a place of great beauty;

- a journey to the Imaginal Realm, where the partners encounter the Third and listen to stories about the Divine Pair;

- a journey into the underworld, where the partners are directly challenged by the shadow aspects of their relationship;

- a ceremony of sacred union, to which the relationship's allies and enemies have all been invited to attend and bring specific gifts.

Other joint practices that enhance visionary imagination are *subtle body scanning* (described in Chapter 4) and *extended deep rhythmic breathing.*[15] When each partner explores the other's subtle body through hand-scanning, spontaneous images sometimes arise that relate to the couple's interactive field and, therefore, to their Third. The hand acts as an antenna, picking up messages from the joint etheric field. Checking out these images with one's partner helps to refine the capacity of visionary imagination to provide a more accurate "picture" of the interactive field.

Extended deep rhythmic or yogic breathing can be performed by itself or in conjunction with any other exercise that stimulates energy interaction and visionary imagination. In either case the breathing work greatly enhances the partners' receptivity to visionary activity.

Council Practices for Enhancing Third Presence

A few council-based practices have been particularly powerful in directly evoking Third Presence.

The Third Pillow Ceremony. In this expansion of dyadic council, another pillow or chair is added as an invitation for the Third to join the ceremony. Just the sight of the "empty" pillow can transform the partners' way of communicating in subtle but significant ways. The talking piece can be placed in front of the Third when its turn comes around and a few moments of silence observed. In addition, if the conversation becomes polarized or blocked, partners can decide to interrupt their dialogue, place the talking piece in front of the third pillow, and listen to the Third. In the silence, they may "hear" a comment or experience a shift in feeling that will refocus the dialogue in a more productive way. As a variation on this practice, either partner can have the option of moving to the empty pillow if he or she feels called to "stand in" for the Third and it is his or her turn to speak. The other partner has the option of commenting on the stand-in's authenticity when the

---

[15] There are many breathing practices that can be used in this connection: for example, the holotropic breath work described in *The Adventure of Self-Discovery: Dimensions of Consciousness and New Perspectives in Psychotherapy and Inner Exploration*, Stanislav Grof, State University of New York Press, 1988.

talking piece comes around. We have found these practices to be a valuable way to receive guidance and increase our sensitivity to the Third's presence.

Other variations of the Third Pillow Ceremony abound, one of which is to ask a close friend or member of the family to take the Third's pillow and act as witness to the dialogue. Sometimes an invitation isn't necessary. There have been occasions when we have been moved by the wisdom of our children speaking in regular family council with an authenticity worthy of our Third.

"Circle of Lovers" practice. We are often involved with gatherings of couples and individuals who have come together with the intention of improving communication in their intimate relationships, expanding their erotic life, and entering Third Presence. In this setting, which we have come to call a "Circle of Lovers," we use a format that extends the Third Pillow Ceremony in a sometimes remarkably effective way.[16] (The Circle of Lovers practice plays a central role in the relationship intensives we conduct at the Ojai Foundation and other locations around the country.)

One of the couples takes their place in the center of the circle formed by the others. The two partners face each other and a third seat is set between them, slightly to one side, as in the Third Pillow Ceremony. The couple begin their dialogue with whatever is "up" for them at the moment, while the rest of the circle sets the intention to witness the couple's interaction as stand-ins for their Third.

As the couple get into their issues, anyone in the outer circle who feels called can take the third pillow, wait for an appropriate pause in the dialogue, and then set the intention to let the voice of the couple's Third speak through them. The Third can offer witness reflections, insights, or other statements that might help the couple see themselves more clearly. Analyzing behavior and

---

[16]Portions of this section overlap with material from *The Way of Council*, Jack Zimmerman in collaboration with Virginia Coyle, Bramble Books, 1996, Chapter 9 and pp. 65-71

giving detailed advice are to be avoided in this practice. In speaking for the couple's Third, brevity is important, and a detached, lighthearted touch is often the most effective. However, Thirds have been known to become confrontative when the partners' self-involvement calls for stronger guidance. After making a statement, the stand-in for the Third returns to the witness circle and the process continues. When the couple feel finished, they leave the center and the entire group offers witness comments on the practice.

The Circle of Lovers can be surprisingly powerful when the group has been together for a while, either during a several-day relationship intensive or when a few couples meet periodically over a long period of time. In the state of heightened perception evoked by this practice, insight flows, defensiveness dissipates, and humor can be a powerful ally. Many strong moments in the Circle of Lovers come to mind...

Didi's experienced tongue took Kenny to task for each one of his failings. Kenny began by directly defending himself, which only whetted Didi's appetite. So he switched to pointing out her shortcomings—particularly her unpredictable swings between angry outbursts and withdrawal. Finally, clutching the talking piece, eyes blazing, she said, "And where is your sexual passion? I want someone who can match mine and take me where I want to go." Kenny slumped on his pillow as Jaquelyn took the Third's seat.

"The woman's knife is sharp," the "Third" began. "She is angry, and her rage turns criticism into a powerful weapon...The difference between an ordinary woman and one in whom the Goddess truly lives is the ability to reflect without overwhelming her man. Any strong woman can find ways to intimidate her man. The woman inspired by the Goddess uses her power to help the man grow. When a woman's fire is allowed to open her own heart before speaking, she serves the Goddess and her man as well."

Didi looked at Jaquelyn and felt a presence beyond the person she had known for years, beyond the familiar champion of women who challenges patriarchal qualities in men, beyond the caller of women to own their power as erotic initiators. Didi *saw* the Third of her relationship for the first time. She lowered her eyes and fell silent. Jaquelyn left the pillow and returned to her seat in the larger circle. Kenny and Didi continued their dialogue, now relatively free of the adversarial and defensive qualities that had dominated it before.

A few months later, Kenny told Jaquelyn that her challenge to Didi had touched something deep in their relationship. "Thanks to you, we're doing much better," he said. Recapturing the power of that transformative moment in the group eluded Jaquelyn. After all, she wasn't the one sitting on the third pillow inside the Circle of Lovers...

Karen and Marty were deeply engaged in a mutual blaming dialogue when the metaphor about dancing first arose. "I want to be able to dance with you," Karen said a little aggressively. "Our relationship doesn't *move*. I want a partner who can hear the music and move with me."

"I hear the music," Marty answered defensively. "But it's different from what *you* hear. God knows, I want to dance, too! I'm fed up with all our fighting. You're never satisfied." They went on for several more minutes, talking about how hard it was to "dance" together and not really listening to each other, before Jack slipped onto the Third's pillow with a playful smile on his face.

"I hear a lot of words about dancing, but I don't observe much listening...Too many words...It's time to move. Would the man and the woman be willing to stop talking and actually dance, right now, silently?" The Third stood, reaching out a hand to each of the partners. They looked a little stunned and momentarily embarrassed, but they knew they needed help and took courage. The

Third moved the pillows and talking piece out of the way, sat down again in the outer circle, and started clapping rhythmically. In a moment the whole witness circle was vigorously beating time.

Karen and Marty danced silently for several minutes, awkwardly at first, then gradually more wildly as they both followed the rhythm of the clapping. By the time they grabbed their pillows and plopped down again in the center, they both were out of breath and smiling broadly. The dialogue shifted a hundred-and-eighty degrees. They acknowledged their stuckness, lack of listening, and desire to feel less judgmental of each other. Within a minute they had dropped into a fruitful dialogue about improving communication during lovemaking.

Patrick and Millie had been engaged in an unproductive dialogue for almost fifteen minutes, during which the Third's pillow remained empty. Millie seemed to be "dying on the vine" for lack of attention from her partner. Words tumbled out of her, followed by expressions of vulnerability and embarrassment at having exposed her loneliness. Patrick responded briefly and without emotion. The rest of us grew restless, as we searched for a doorway through which their Third could enter. Finally, Robbie, the youngest of the men in the circle, moved to the empty pillow. In an almost offhand voice he said, "I wonder if the woman would be willing to look at the man without speaking for a few minutes. Perhaps then she would *see* him with new eyes."

As Robbie returned to his seat, Millie put the talking piece down in front of her and stopped talking. From where she sat (and several others of us directly behind her), Patrick's head was silhouetted against the bright sunlight streaming in through the windows. Millie stared at Patrick for several minutes, squinting to make out his features in the glare of the late afternoon sun. Time seemed to stand still. Our restlessness dropped away. Millie finally broke the silence.

"You have a glow around you that extends beyond the glare. I see an old soul, a mystic, perhaps a monk from an earlier time. He has moved beyond words, finding them inadequate to describe what he has learned during his long life journey." (We found out later that some of us shared the basic tone of Millie's insights.) "You are a teacher, a wise and silent teacher, from whom I have much to learn. I have never seen the God in you before."

Patrick smiled but didn't respond. Millie spoke briefly one more time before they both left their place in the center of the circle. A few minutes later, Millie concluded the full witness circle with a summary of her experience: "A part of my heart has been closed to you all these years, because I haven't recognized who you are. I'm grateful to our Third for helping me to *see*. I hope this experience doesn't slip away, as we pick up the threads of our regular life together." A chorus of smiling, nodding heads echoed Millie's prayer...

Sheila and Lindsay brought their longstanding debate about having a child into the circle. He was eager to be a father; at forty and in marginal health, she was ambivalent. The dialogue soon became an elaboration of how little either of their needs was being met in the relationship. Their Third—disguised as Jaquelyn—finally came to the rescue. "There are already two children here who need a lot of caring before another child can be conceived," was all she said. Sheila and Lindsay's laughter shifted the level of their dialogue entirely. Although it took several more months, they finally resolved the issue in favor of not becoming parents.

By witnessing the process and occasionally standing in for another couple's Third, each member of the circle develops the ability to enter Third Presence in his or her own relationship. The couple in the center receive helpful reflections to the degree that members of the witness circle are able to observe the couple's interaction objectively and use their visionary imagination creatively.

Over the years, this practice has taught us a lot about the art of witnessing and recognizing the authentic voice of Third Presence. The value of this expanded Third Pillow Ceremony obviously depends on the group's level of astuteness, creativity, and ability to surrender personal needs in order to serve the couple in the center. Yet we have found that the nature of the Third's presence from group to group is remarkably consistent. In general, we have found that the Third speaks in one of three modes:

As a witness. This mode includes simple reflection, both about the content of the relationship and the process of communication (most often, the quality of listening). The Third is passionate about the need for listening attentively and is sometimes confrontative with couples who are so self-preoccupied that they can't hear each other. In witnessing the content of relationships, the Third most often uses images and analogies to describe patterns of behavior, rather than intervening analytically or giving direct advice.

"The man and the woman remind me of debaters who are arguing which gender has the hardest road to travel" might be the Third's opening comment to a couple deeply engaged with gender issues. "You might pretend that the debate is over now, the judges have decided it was a draw, and it's time to leave the hall and have dinner together. How would you feel as you walk out into a balmy, starry night? What might the evening have in store for you?"

As an innovator of spontaneous ceremonies and playful exercises. Sometimes reflection is not sufficient to break old patterns and set new intentions. Recognizing that a more active and creative mode of intervention is called for, the Third might suggest a role-playing exercise or a playful game to shift the mood and break the logjam.

Jeannie and Tony were overwhelmed by work and parenting two girls, ages five and nine. Their erotic life was virtually dead on the vine and Jeannie had sunk into a pattern of silent stoic despair. Tony was so busy with his medical practice that he hardly noticed the absence of any personal passion in his marriage. He didn't have a clue about why Jeannie was so depressed and withdrawn. Jeannie had lost the ability to tell Tony how miserable she felt and what she wanted. We witnessed them avoid any real contact for thirty minutes (during which many stand-ins for their Third did what they could to reflect the obvious need for spending more quality time together).

Suddenly, an inspired Jaquelyn slipped into the third pillow. "Tell me about your nine-year-old daughter," she asked Jeannie. The woman's face broke into a smile for the first time as she described a bright and precocious young lady, whom she obviously loved more than life itself. "Let's play a little game," the Third went on. "Suppose for a moment you become your daughter and look at your relationship with Tony through her nine-year-old eyes. Tell us what you see."

Jeannie's smile slowly turned into a frown and then dissolved in sadness. In a shaky voice—that sounded authentically young— we heard a clear and deeply felt description of the paralyzed marriage we had been witnessing. Jeannie's moving story got Tony's attention. Their dialogue resumed as the Third rejoined the circle. Now the genie was out of the bottle. We witnessed an increase in truth-telling and the beginning of real communication that called in several other useful reflections.

Occasionally, the Third will ask the couple if they are willing to create a ceremony of recommitment, including vows that speak to the present challenges of their partnership. Once, a couple actually decided to get married during the Circle of Lovers practice. There have also been rites of passage for relationships entering new phases: the birth of a child, the last teenager leaving home, starting a new life in another state, launching a visionary project in the world, and in a few instances, moving out of the relationship into a much needed state of separation. Sometimes the Third quotes a poem or saying that describes some aspect of their relationship or asks each of the partners to make up one spontaneously.

As an entity imitating human emotions. Another effective way the Third can enter is by "pretending" it has strong humanlike emotions and sharing how it feels in the moment to be the couple's visionary guide.

[*with a touch of despair*] "Your voices are so faint, I can hardly hear you." (For a couple whose erotic life had all but disappeared.)

[*with a touch of anger*] "The man and the woman are so busy trying to get their own needs met that I am left to wait, unnourished. Your relationship has needs too." (This sentiment is frequently shared by Thirds with couples who are so self-involved that they are completely unable to see the transcendent possibilities in their relationship.)

[*with head in hands and a voice full of anguish*] "Oh...Oh..." (For a couple so overwhelmed with their individual troubles that they had left their relationship quite unattended.)

[*with great warmth and appreciation*] "I have been waiting a long time for this moment!" (For partners who had been neglecting their erotic life and suddenly came to realize how important it was to them.)

The sense of spirit that often infuses the Third Pillow Ceremony is similar to what the Quakers call the "Third Way." In regard to resolving conflict through dialogue, they say (paraphrasing): "There is the truth you bring, and the truth I bring—and, finally, there is the truth of the Third Way." What we have been calling the Third Presence in intimate relationship is related to exploring the Third Way in open-hearted Quaker dialogue.

We used Third Pillow Councils many times during our collaboration on this book to solidify our joint vision and clarify the somewhat different perspectives we brought to the writing. On most of these occasions we were able to enter Third Presence and reach the lucidity we sought. Sometimes we were guided directly by what we heard from our otherworldly friend; sometimes we were sent back to the drawing board without explicit directions. Those councils made it clear that our Third is quite literally a coauthor of this book.

The Therapist as Stand-in for the Third

Our explorations of Third Presence have also transformed the way we counsel couples in our private practice. Jack remembers one of the earliest experiences that opened the door to our working in this manner.

Roger and Dee both saw their relationship as problematical and, with some regularity, seriously questioned whether they should continue. Despite their strong sexual connection, they couldn't understand why they held onto their relationship in the face of all the difficulties.

During a particularly difficult therapeutic session, I found myself wanting to take the perspective of their Third, rather than continuing along the more conventional lines that were proving ineffective. I set the intention silently and waited to see what would happen. A few moments later I sensed a shift in my perception and mood. I felt activated, even optimistic, although Roger and Dee were engaged in an angry argument at the time. There was a remarkable contrast between my perceptions as a stand-in for their Third and my previous despairing feelings as their therapist.

Within a few minutes I realized that the transcendent dimension of their relationship had been initiated sometime in the past, despite the many thorny issues that separated them. Since neither of them was aware of this awakening, I decided to take the leap and speak as their Third without telling them what I was doing.

We all noticed the shift in mood. Over the next hour, the Third helped them to see how the challenges of their journey were perfectly designed to illuminate the difficult but important issues each of them had to face as individuals. The Third also spoke of their love with greater passion and authority than I had been able to muster as counselor. For a few moments Roger and Dee clearly saw the yet untapped power of their erotic connection. They stopped fighting, listened for a while, and then continued their dialogue with a lot less attachment to their old positions. A distinct increase in mutual respect and a lessening of pain and despair about their difficulties in communicating were apparent.

Witnessing a couple by standing in for their Third during conjoint counseling sessions has become an illuminating practice for both of us. It has increased the insight and transformative power of our work and, of course, been invaluable in understanding the way the Third manifests in our own relationship.

Six
Preparing for Sexual Communion

We pull the rain in around us
Like a wet curtain of sound for our lovemaking
At first gentle, caressing the blue metal roof
Then an hour later, in perfect passionate rhythm
Sheets of pounding water sweep us into surrender

This time, more than two people making love
We are a duet created by gifted musicians
Who, playing wet and easy
Like the countless fingers on the blue roof
Make music we have never heard before
We are children in a secret rain garden
Every movement awakening wonder and delight
Fascinated beyond images and old stories
Discovering anew how our bodies belong
To both earth and heaven

We have the rain to thank
For quieting all our voices
Save the simple song of two souls in love
And later, sleepy, still safe inside the curtain
We remember the rain is only part of the mystery

*T*he sexual life of a relationship flourishes when each of the lovers has developed a healthy awareness of other, an ongoing willingness to move beyond self-preoccupation, and an interest in exploring the Imaginal Realm through the medium of visionary imagination. With this in mind, we can identify three stages in the natural progression of sexual maturity.

- *Stage 1*: Primary focus on *personal gratification*, physically and emotionally.

- *Stage 2*: Expanded focus on physical and emotional *gratification of self and partner*.

- *Stage 3*: Simultaneous awareness of self, other, and the intermingling of subtle bodies leads to the *practice of sexual communion*. Gratification now depends largely on the creative use of visionary imagination and the degree to which the lovers can access Third Presence. Lovemaking in this stage is guided by the Third as a celebration of the Divine Pair.

A good way to visualize these stages is as three concentric circles, each larger than and including the preceding one. Thus, becoming significantly aware of your partner in stage 2 is not at the expense of self-gratification. Rather, personal pleasure now becomes inseparable from the capacity to please your partner. Becoming aware of Third Presence during stage 3 does not imply less focus on your partner or yourself. On the contrary, since the Third is an interweaving of you and your partner's subtle bodies, sensitivity to both your physical bodies and etheric fields is essential to being in the Third's presence. The basic challenge of stage 3 is to be attentive enough to function on several levels of consciousness simultaneously.

Couples move through these stages as a result of both intentional and spontaneous growth experiences. Maturation rarely progresses smoothly. The process usually follows the familiar "two steps forward, one step back." Naturally, boundaries between the stages are not sharply drawn. Partners centered in the first stage might have a powerful mutual experience of each other during a particularly passionate sexual encounter and so be inspired to begin to discover the joys of the next stage. Similarly, in a mature stage-2 relationship, when the couple is learning to prolong the period of lovemaking prior to reaching physical climax, there may well be moments of stage-3 sexuality.

Intentional development means that the partners' "walk their talk" about expanding their sexual life. This means setting aside regular time for sexual exploration and open discussions about sexuality. Many of the exercises offered in previous chapters provide opportunities for couples in stages 1 and 2 to intentionally prepare the way for the practices of sexual communion.

In Chapter 2 we discussed the underlying pattern of moving from a state of physical, emotional, and mental tension to a momentary release of this tension through orgasmic sexuality. The practice of sexual communion is based on freeing lovemaking from the *obligation* to be a primary source of tension-release through a *pattern* of orgasmic discharge. In fact, stage-3 sexuality does usually release physical, emotional, and mental tension in subtle ways, but principally as a secondary effect of expanded awareness and not as a primary goal. Using council and other practices that will be described shortly, the challenge is to deal with tension wherever it arises in the relationship and so clear the air as much as possible before lovemaking.

As we have emphasized, transcending relationships require the continual monitoring and resolution of gender biases and imbalances. This is particularly true of couples making the transition from stage 2 to stage 3. The flexibility and openness required to enjoy the delights of sexual communion are seriously inhibited by attachments to traditional male/female sexual roles and expectations. In particular, women need to awaken their innate capacity for penetration/initiation to balance the receptive/magnetic aspects of eroticism more commonly expected of them. Conversely, men need to awaken their innate receptive/magnetic capabilities to balance the initiatory, penetrating sexuality traditionally expected of them. In addition, sexual maturity requires that couples free themselves from trying to meet current cultural standards of performance (mostly the man's burden) and sexual attractiveness (mostly the woman's).

The challenges of attaining a more mature sexual life are indeed formidable. But, above all, we need remind ourselves that the path to sexual communion is created with openings of the heart. When all is said and done, the sexual techniques and activities described in this and the following chapter are simply more conscious ways to make love.

෨

Awakening Love's Body

The practices of sexual communion rest on a foundation of body consciousness. In a highly developed erotic person, sensual and sexual awareness is not focused primarily on the genitals but, rather, touches every cell, informs the mind, and permeates the emotions. These unusual individuals can enter a state of creativity and heightened expression during lovemaking that might be called "erotic grace." In non-sexual as well as sexual activities, they experience a more vital state of body awareness that encourages good health and heightens their interactions with others. Conversely, a substantial lack of erotic aliveness can contribute to depression and illness, as well as difficulties with intimacy and creative expression.

A body that has been awakened to its full erotic potential we call a manifestation of "Love's Body." Love's Body transforms the yearning for wholeness—the "ache for love"—into a merging of flesh and spirit that can, but need not, result in an act of sexual love.

In counseling couples over the years, as well as in our own relationship, we have explored many ways to awaken the erotic body-awareness that is potential in all of us. These approaches fall into several categories: education and therapy, body and genital acceptance, movement, pelvic exercises, and visionary imagination during lovemaking.

Education and therapy. There are many excellent books with explicit diagrams and a wealth of detail to assist anyone willing to learn about sexuality.[1] An increasing number of men's and women's groups (at least in urban areas), workshops for couples and singles, and many therapeutic modalities are available that focus on sexual functioning.

Therapy is often helpful when major wounds in early childhood have caused sexual inhibition and excessive fear of intimacy. However, starting with Masters and Johnson's pioneering work in behavioral sexual therapy,[2] it has become increasingly clear that many dysfunctional behaviors can be reduced or eliminated without deep insight-oriented therapy. As people are taught how to function more effectively—in part through receiving information, permission, and direction by respected friends, workshop leaders, authors, etc.—their self-esteem and sexual capacity can

---

[1] We mention just a few that are perhaps less well known: *The Art of Sexual Ecstasy: The Path of Sacred Sexuality for Western Lovers*, Margo Anand, J. P. Tarcher, 1989; and *Sexual Energy Ecstasy: A Practical Guide to Lovemaking Secrets of the East and West*, David and Ellen Ramsdale, Peak Skill Publishing, 1985.
[2] *Human Sexual Response*, William Masters and Virginia Johnson, Little Brown & Co., 1966.

often improve without having to process a lot of early family dynamics in a therapeutic environment.

Body and genital acceptance. A relationship will support the awakening of Love's Body in both partners if they feel safe enough to talk about the sensitive issues surrounding body-image and sexuality. Feelings and attitudes need to be shared honestly and compassionately in a way that helps clarify sexual misunderstandings and releases the pain of self-consciousness. Since body-image usually involves early imprinting, being insensitive or judgmental of one's partner in this area can reopen old wounds.

For example, many women suffer with feelings of being too fat, too skinny, too short, too tall, too hairy, or (almost universally) simply not beautiful enough. They worry that their breasts are saggy, small, large, asymmetrical, or that the nipples are too smooth, protruding, pigmented, etc., etc. They frequently fear men will find their genitals frightening or offensive.

Men often express concern about their height and the size, shape, and function of their penises. Men also worry about their muscle development and having too much or not enough hair on their face or body. Baldness is a particularly distressing problem for many men (and a few women). Adolescents of both sexes worry even more about their anatomy, not to mention the problems of acne, social awkwardness, and confusion about sexual identity.

It is liberating for men and women to express their fears openly in same-sex groups and learn that almost everyone has worries about the imperfections of his or her body.[3] It is particularly reassuring to hear those we admire admit they have dreaded undressing in front of a sexual partner at times because they felt self-conscious about their body. After the group has met for a while, this kind of sharing is often accompanied by a great deal of humor as well as compassion for oneself and others. To appreciate that we can be insecure about our physiology yet still be both loving and lovable is a major step towards awakening Love's Body.

[3] This practice is a regular part of our relationship intensives at the Ojai Foundation.

Most important, couples need to communicate intimately about sensitive body-image and sexual issues in dyadic council. Eventually it is unnecessary to set themes for these councils, but to get the ball rolling, the following questions and topics may help to establish a new level of honesty and openness.

- What parts of your body do you particularly like? What parts do you dislike? Have these feelings changed since you were young? How has your present sexual relationship affected these likes and dislikes?

- Describe an incident when a friend or family member said something about your body that hurt your feelings.

- What parts of your body are the most sensitive to erotic arousal? What factors affect this sensitivity (such as gentleness of touch, temperature, mood)?

- What parts of your partner's body are you most attracted to? What parts are easily aroused? Do any parts seem generally unresponsive? What factors seem to affect your partner's pleasure and capacity to be aroused?

- What works well in your lovemaking now? In what areas has there been the most improvement (e.g., anticipation, setting the scene, foreplay, oral sex, verbal communication, manual stimulation, penetration, orgasm, timing, pace, experimentation, acknowledgment)?

- In what areas would you like to see improvement?

- Do you have any goals for your sexual life? Wild fantasies?

- Do people other than your partner enter your mind and/or fantasies during sexual activity?

- How do alcohol and other substances affect your sexual presence and that of your partner? What are your feelings about using substances to ease inhibitions and increase body-mind sexual presence?

- How do you feel about aging in relationship to your sexuality?

Movement. Enjoying how one's body functions outside the sexual arena can be of great assistance in developing expanded erotic capacity. Generally this means getting enough sleep, eating well, exercising, and learning how to move in a more conscious way. Although we all know that vigorous body movement, done in moderation, can be helpful, strenuous exercise is often *not* the most appropriate activity for awakening Love's Body. Rather, we have found that certain pelvic muscle exercises and gentle fluctuations of the spine and pelvis, called "undulations," can enhance erotic movements, increase pelvic awareness, and facilitate the flow of sexual energy in the body.

Undulation was originally introduced to us by our dear friend Emilie Conrad Da'oud as part of a movement awareness process she developed, called *Continuum.*[4] In a standing, sitting, or reclining position, one starts by slightly arching the spine with the chest forward and the head tilted back. Then the spine is slowly and gently flexed to produce a subtle wavelike movement that culminates with the head tilted forward and down and the pelvis thrust forward and up. The movement is repeated in a continuous undulating cycle that becomes more wavelike as the spine becomes increasingly supple. Although not necessarily the goal of the exercise when used as part of Continuum, with time and practice, these movements gain increasing subtlety until just a slight, almost undetectable, forward tilt of the pelvis can initiate an undulating sensation and awareness of sexual energy throughout the body.

---

[4]Continuum is a series of movement, meditation, breath, and sound practices that awaken "cellular consciousness" and can play a remarkable role in healing body rigidity, injury, and even paralysis. The Continuum studio is located in Santa Monica, California.

Kegel exercises. A direct approach to arousing Love's Body genitally involves the use of the pelvic Kegel exercises that were developed originally to heal bladder incontinence.[5] The Kegels strengthen the pubococcygeus muscles, which are important for bladder and urethral function. The pubococcygeus surrounds not only the urethra but also the anus and, in women, the outer portion of the vagina. These muscles stop defecation and the flow of urine as well as support the internal sexual anatomy and affect the sensation of orgasm.

The technique is basically the same for both men and women: repeatedly contract the pubococcygeus muscles for a few seconds, as if one were interrupting urination or holding back stool, and then release. The number of contractions should be gradually increased to sixty or eighty, with rests in between each group of twenty. The contraction/release sequence can also be performed rapidly for additional strengthening. It is suggested that fast and slow contractions be alternated during each of three exercise periods each day. Increased genital awareness and control, which are central to the development of Love's Body, are often apparent after about four to six weeks. Many have found that the Kegel exercises in conjunction with the undulations provide a valuable source of energy for improving health and creative expression, as well as for sexual activity.

A regular practice of this kind can lead to a highly localized physical awareness that can be described as *cellular consciousness*. In this state, our five senses seem to be present in every cell (in fact, they are!), creating an enhanced level of body awareness generally and expanding the pleasure of erotic activities in particular. As cellular consciousness increases, emotional and mental inhibitions gradually diminish and the flow of sexual energy increases throughout the body. This increased flow supports sexual practices during which orgasm is consciously and deliciously delayed or even avoided entirely. The capacity to experience a

---

[5] See the discussion in Chapter 2.

strong current of sexual energy, without the need to release through discharge, in turn further awakens Love's Body.

Visionary imagination during lovemaking. Being able to consciously delay or avoid discharging during lovemaking intensifies the interpenetration of the subtle bodies and thereby invites the couple to enter Third Presence and explore the Imaginal Realm. Contact with this expanded level of consciousness becomes more direct, vibrant, and loving. As a consequence, the partners' visionary capacities grow until their lovemaking takes on a larger-than-life mythical quality. How many lovers have felt like Adam and Eve in the garden making love for the first time!

Conversely, increased contact with the mysteries of the Imaginal Realm shifts more of the partners' awareness to their subtle bodies, allowing them to enjoy an abundance of sexual energy and still remain "on the edge." This, in turn, further heightens the couple's visionary imagination and so their sexual practice continues growing more pleasurable and illuminating.

☯

The Practice of Sexual Communion

For some people the word *ceremony* conjures up meaningless rituals, blind adherence to dogma, or the dangers of cults. As justified as these associations may be in particular situations, the resulting fear and widespread aversion to ceremony in our culture is a classic example of throwing away the baby with the bathwater. By avoiding ceremony, we disown a basic human instinct as old as the shamanic tradition, and we forfeit an enormous source of creative power for personal transformation and healing.[6] Furthermore, rejection of ceremonial practices activates a vicious cycle. Lacking opportunities for conscious expression, the ceremonial

---

[6] For example, see *Shaman: The Wounded Healer*, Joan Halifax, Thames & Hudson Ltd., 1982; *The Shaman's Doorway: Opening Imagination to Power and Myth*, Stephen Larsen, Harper and Row, 1988; and *The Ceremonial Circle*, Sedonia Cahill and Joshua Halpern, HarperCollins, 1990.

instinct emerges in unconscious, violent ways, such as in urban gangs or (ironically) in perilous cults led by demagogues. The challenge for each of us is to manifest our natural instinct for creating ceremony in a way that is authentic, at times spontaneous, and always consistent with personal freedom and empowerment.

The practice of sexual communion lends itself delightfully to the expression of ceremonial instincts. We can reawaken the numinous and joyous elements of authentic ceremony by approaching a time of lovemaking with heightened sensory awareness, an open mind, and a curiosity about connecting with the Mystery. Unlike habitual sexual patterning (particularly when it is unconscious), the co-creation of sexual ceremony does not inhibit spontaneity but rather *invites* it on a deeper level. In fact, authentic sexual ceremonies invariably transcend the dampening effects of premeditation, since they are open to the unpredictable blessings of Eros.

An important prerequisite to establishing a satisfying practice of sexual communion is to set aside sufficient time to truly "make" (that is, *create*) love. Choosing the last twenty minutes of a long, exhausting day provides a poor setting for the practice. The inspiration and creativity of sexual communion flower in the absence of time restraints. Since they rarely occur in the midst of life's ordinary patterns, interludes of at least two or three hours need to be set aside. Then arrangements can be made to take care of children, animals, important chores, etc., and the excitement of anticipation has a chance to work its magic.

For some couples making love in the morning or during the magical light of late afternoon can heighten the senses and avoid end-of- day fatigue. For others the evening may promise a fuller embrace of the Mystery, be more practical, or offer sleep as a welcomed final portion of the ceremony. If a couple are used to one time of day, experimenting with another opens up new opportunities. Naturally, the timing of sexual interludes shifts with mood and the change of seasons.

Setting the Scene

Giving attention to creating an environment conducive to lovemaking is worth the time and trouble. For most people, privacy is a high priority. Knowing no one will interrupt frees the mind from concerns that may inhibit the subtleties of the practice. Turn off the phone (unless that produces more anxiety). If older children are around, explain to them you need a few hours to be alone with each other. If they ask questions, give them straight answers, appropriate to their age and circumstances. In most family situations it is beneficial that children learn to respect their parents' desire to have private time together.

Take a while to create a feeling of *spaciousness and comfort*. A small room can be made to feel larger if the clutter is removed. Warming the room in winter for an hour before coming together, or using a fireplace if one is lucky enough to have one, heightens the senses. Candles, flowers, or incense add important touches for many couples. Often music helps to produce a relaxing environment, but be aware that visionary imagination and other aspects of the practice can be unpredictably influenced by sound. Experiment! A large blanket and a few small pillows can make the outdoors a literal bower of bliss. The sounds of nature often stir the imagination and are rarely intrusive. Whatever the basic environment the couple start with, it is the use of imagination and attention given to creating the setting that really matter.

Clearing the Field

The couple's abilities to awaken visionary imagination and remain on the edge are both enhanced by dealing with mental, emotional, and physical obstructions before lovemaking actually begins. If either partner is consciously holding potentially distracting feelings, a clearing council is recommended at the beginning of the erotic interlude.

The increased awareness that arises out of practices of sexual communion may also open partners to seeing more of their shadow sides. Difficult material that surfaces during lovemaking may cause a subtle "leaving" of the body-mind or a kind of sleepiness that adversely affects sexual functioning. The challenge is not to see such occurrences as sexual failures but as opportunities for doing more refined shadow work and thus strengthening the relationship. This aspect of sexual communion can be likened to the innovative alchemist looking for raw material (disowned aspects of oneself) to turn into gold (more conscious love). Shifting into an informal clearing council in the midst of lovemaking is certainly a viable alternative to ignoring the reality of what's happening.

The sharing of dreams, the embrace meditation, and many of the energy exchange practices provide a supportive prelude to sexual communion. The creative use of these practices is an essential part of the orchestration of mature lovemaking. For example, if either partner is feeling contracted, stressed, or physically debilitated, the embrace meditation can be used to reduce tension and reawaken both partners to visionary collaboration. A simple foot massage can work wonders as a remedy for feeling less than fully present in one's body.

Many couples enjoy the practice of bathing before lovemaking, either together or separately. Others prefer the stimulus of body scents and the natural skin oils that bathing diminishes. Communicating personal preferences about this often sensitive area is important. Smell is considered by many the most primitive of our physical senses and often conjures up old memories and strong feelings. If oral/genital contact is to be part of the couple's lovemaking, then smell and taste both become significant matters to discuss. Conscious attention to breath odor is also important. We know of several loving relationships whose sexual life was seriously compromised by reactions to breath or body secretion odors.

Most couples tend to avoid making love during the woman's menstrual cycle, although we have known a few for whom this interval offers a particularly attractive time for sexual intimacy. In certain traditions (Orthodox Judaism, for example), menstruation is seen as a time when women are in need of a hiatus from their usual intimate or ceremonial contact with men. Naturally, such customs can always be honored as part of the couple's sexual practice, or the partners can develop their own way of dealing with the menstrual cycle. For example, an extended embrace meditation, during which the couple use their visionary imagination to image sexual union, provides an alternative to intercourse during this time.

Traditional erotic ceremonies sometimes included small amounts of wine and specially prepared foods. Some people find hunger distracting and prefer to eat lightly an hour or two before lovemaking begins. Others enjoy the edge that being slightly hungry creates and are more alert when their digestive system is not processing a meal. More than small amounts of alcohol and food during or just before sexual communion usually hinder the subtle mind-body awareness on which the practice thrives. Half a glass of wine may help some people relax, but several glasses will usually inhibit the flow of sexual energy. As always, innovation and variation are the spices of sexual life.

Maintaining Focus

The abilities to stay focused and relaxed in mind and body are strong allies of sexual communion. Being mindful of intention, breathing, and visual imagery are helpful in this regard.

Before the start of lovemaking, *setting the intention together* to delay or avoid discharge provides a point of reference for the entire practice and supports the ability of both partners to relax as arousal intensifies. If the couple's intentions are vague or there is ambivalence as lovemaking begins, tension may develop and the practice is more likely to be aborted by unconscious movement towards discharge. Having a preliminary council is often a good way to clarify and reinforce the partners' intentions.

Many people become unconscious of their *breathing* during lovemaking, at which time it commonly becomes rapid and shallow as climax approaches. A primary goal in sexual communion is to stay aware of one's breathing and maintain a steady, relaxed intake of oxygen. In this respect, sexual communion is similar to traditional meditation, which often stresses conscious attention to the breath as a primary part of the discipline.[7]

Becoming aware of the breath is particularly helpful for men in extending the interval of sexual excitement and avoiding an accidental rush to climax. Slowing down the breathing can break habitual patterns and supports stretching out the ascent towards orgasm. Particularly when combined with visual imagery, consciously regulating the breath affords an effective and direct way of expanding and prolonging arousal.

For many individuals sexual arousal comes in waves, with the time between peaks depending on the physical pace and rhythm of the lovemaking. An important time for implementing conscious breathing is during the build-up of one of these waves. When one is able to breathe "through" the wave (possibly making exuberant sounds at the same time), the movement towards climax is slowed and one has the feeling of gliding into a new, more relaxed state of surrender and awareness. Being able to respond to intense arousal in this way often releases a surge of love for one's partner and greater awareness of Third Presence. As the practice evolves, the waves of arousal often occur more frequently and become more subtle, culminating in a gently undulating state of heightened awareness.

Imagery

The activation of visionary imagination during sexual communion provides opportunities for using imagery (in conjunction with breath awareness) to extend the time of heightened arousal.

---

[7] For a full discussion of breathing during sexual activity, see *The Art of Sexual Ecstasy: The Path of Sacred Sexuality for Western Lovers*, Margo Anand, J.P. Tarcher Inc., 1989.

Below we offer imagery that involves the seven chakras. Sensual images and traditional representations of ecstatic lovemaking (such as depicted in Tibetan tankas) are delightful alternatives. Of course, image/breath exercises can also be practiced at times other than during lovemaking.

- Imagine that your inhalation comes through the sexual center and, on each exhale, redistributes the intense focus of sexual energy from the genital area to other parts of the body. Imagine the flow moving down your legs and out the bottom of your feet into the earth. With each exhalation visualize the sexual energy rising up from the genitals along the spine, igniting the centers associated with the abdomen, heart, throat, brow, and crown.

- Imagine an energy pathway connecting your partner's root and crown chakras to your root and crown, respectively, with the remaining parts of the loop formed by your two spinal columns. On each inhale move the energy from your root and sexual centers up the spine and out the top of your head. On the exhale imagine the flow descending into your partner's spine, moving through all his or her upper centers to the root and then across the lower part of the loop into your own root chakra.[8] Experiment with imaging the flow circulating in the opposite direction to see which enables you to sustain the heightened arousal more readily. (If both partners use this visualization at the same time, the energy usually will be felt moving in both directions simultaneously.)

- Imagine the penis inside the sheath of the vagina becoming a source of light that permeates both your physical and subtle bodies. The light can be imagined

---

[8] The breath acts as an "energy pump" that keeps the flow moving in the loop, thereby avoiding a significant genital build-up.

as pulsating outward with each exhale. (When only subtle adjustments are needed to keep from moving into climax, visualizations of this kind can be used without breath coordination.)

- [for men] Let the intense feelings of pleasure and arousal in your genitals slowly spread outward, until your entire body becomes a giant phallus penetrating your partner's etheric field.

- [for women] Let the focus of pleasure and arousal in your genitals slowly expand, opening outward until your entire body is a large exotic flower embracing your partner.

- Imagine your and your partner's sexual chakras as the transmitting and receiving centers for the physical chemistry in your relationship. Let your hearts play the same role for the spiritual chemistry. Shift the focus of your attention (with or without breath coordination) from the physical to the spiritual connection between you and your partner, until you find a balance that permits maintaining arousal without climaxing.

- Imagine your subtle bodies interpenetrating and then being bathed in spirit emanations from the Divine Pair. Allow yourselves to feel the heightened presence of the Third and be open to its guidance.

- Imagine that you and your partner are in the Temple of the Third, celebrating with your devoted ally. Imagine the scene, giving attention to the physical details of the celebration.

Of course, imaging can be used to heighten and concentrate physical arousal in the genitals as well as to moderate and diffuse it. If the man loses his erection, for example, or either partner becomes distracted from the lovemaking, then energy can be drawn into the genital area through a combination of breathing and imagery.

Manifesting the intention to delay or forgo orgasmic discharge takes time and experimentation, the extent varying greatly from couple to couple. In the early stages of the exploration, there is usually a strong feeling of holding back and perhaps some awkwardness and self-consciousness. If one is drawn into climax, we suggest releasing fully without judgment or recrimination, staying as conscious as possible throughout the process. There are no failures. Learn what you can and try again. One cannot ask for more delightful experimentation.

As the ability to relax and maintain control develops, the sense of restraint usually fades and the focus shifts from avoiding old patterns to exploring the new practice. Gradually the conscious use of breath and imagery becomes less necessary and the couple's visionary imagination can be made more available for spontaneous exploration of the Imaginal Realm.

We have found that using images of other sexual partners to enhance arousal is, for most couples, inconsistent with the practice of sexual communion. Ultimately, the heart of the practice is to sense one's partner as divine, which suggests that the man sees his lover as all women and the woman embraces her man as all men. For most people, bringing in images of other partners fragments this vision of wholeness.

Verbal Communication

For many couples, the use of visionary imagination during lovemaking is enhanced by verbal interplay. Sharing images, humor, newly made discoveries and, of course, expressions of love can help a couple to become more aware of the subtler movements of their sexual energy.

However, some people (men more than women, in our experience) find talking during sex difficult. They tell us that it moves them into their heads and diminishes attention to bodily pleasures. Our response is that every aspect of consciousness is invited to the celebration of sexual communion, the head most definitely included! If verbal communication is put at the disposal of the couple's visionary imagination, then it should not be a distraction but rather an elaboration and amplification of what is happening nonverbally. As in other aspects of the practice, creative erotic conversation requires practice and experimentation to overcome silence or old verbal patterns. Talking about the matter during a preliminary council is often helpful.

One approach is for partners to share images and body sensations in the spirit of dreamsharing. For example:

- "The boundary between our bodies is dissolving…"

- "I've entered an otherworldly garden…You're there…I don't have to see you to know where you are…"

- "I see us slowly approaching each other, looking into each other's eyes. We're still a ways apart, but I feel our intermingling…It's sweet, tangible…"

- "When you're inside me like this, I lose all boundaries…We fit perfectly…"

- "I'm seeing geometric shapes filled with light…Each wave of energy changes the colors…"

- "We're in another world, where we know each other's thoughts…Now I can't hide how much I love you…"

- "Who are you…a goddess, a sorceress, a priestess of Eros?"

- "We've never been here before…We're in the presence of the Mystery…"

- "You fill me with a strong golden light…It flows through every cell in my body…We are conceiving a Divine Child…"

- "We're in the Temple of our Third...being initiated..."

- "I see an eternal pair...They look at us in a knowing way...They ask us to come closer...Are we ready?"

- "I have never felt such love...We are dissolving into the heart of it...We are dying..."

Caressing

A common complaint in many relationships—particularly from women—is that there isn't enough caressing, kissing, or foreplay. When orgasm is the primary goal of lovemaking, these activities tend to be seen as preliminaries and given less emphasis. Much has been written in recent years about this topic and invariably the advice is for couples to spend more time exploring each other's bodies before genital contact. In one renowned survey a majority of women, when faced with the hypothetical choice between sexual intercourse and being held in a long, tender embrace, overwhelmingly chose the latter.[9]

As the emphasis moves away from orgasm, the arts of caressing and kissing take on more importance in the relationship—not primarily as preparation for what is to follow but *as expressions of erotic love in their own right.*

Some people (again, particularly women) feel that a deep, loving kiss can be more intimate than making love. Apart from the incredible neurological sensitivity of the lips and mouth, perhaps this is because we are generally more conscious of our mouths than our genitals. A loving kiss can be a mutual surrender of much of what we identify as uniquely ourselves—our voice, our place of taking in nourishment. Some couples see the mouth as a bisexual organ complete with labia (lips), articulate phallus (tongue), and the fluids of lubrication. For them, kissing provides

---

[9] In November of 1984, syndicated advice columnist Ann Landers asked her female readers the following question: "Would you be content to be held close and treated tenderly and forget about 'the act'?" Over 72 percent of some 90,000 women chose being held over intercourse.

an opportunity to subtly shift and even transcend the biological aspects of gender identities.

Kissing, despite its ubiquity, may be one of the most neglected arts in our culture. Useful descriptions of kissing in nonfictional literature are rare.[10] Our own councils about kissing have involved issues of firmness (don't get "mushy" and go unconscious), wetness (don't drown me), tongue activity (be gentle and playful), nibbling (take an exploratory journey), biting (exciting, but don't draw blood), and breathing (don't forget to). We have enjoyed many erotic pilgrimages during which a prolonged kiss was one of the highlights of the evening.

Communicating regularly with your partner about caressing is important. Moods and inclinations change. There are times when the lightest touch is delightful and other occasions when greater pressure is more exciting. Think of caressing as "finger-body" communication to be continually refined until a mutually satisfying state is achieved. Hand-scanning each other's subtle bodies (being sure not to touch) is a good way to initiate a period of caressing. If awareness of the subtle body can be maintained even after making physical contact, then caressing becomes a multidimensional experience.

Since the major energy centers lie near the spinal axis, caressing the spine is another excellent way to stimulate your partner's esoteric and physical anatomy at the same time. The lower back is a highly sensitive erogenous area for many people. Gentle but firm massaging of the region near the hips where the buttocks begin to swell (about three or four inches from the spine) can be remarkably arousing. Our experience in stimulating this area leaves no doubt as to why it is called "the Gates of Heaven" in Eastern tradition. The middle of the upper back is another area of great sensitivity. Firm pressure here on both sides of the spine helps

---

[10] *Sexual Secrets: The Alchemy of Ecstasy*, Nik Douglas and Penny Slinger, Destiny Books, 1979, pp. 193-195.

one's partner make the shift from ordinary reality to the Imaginal Realm.

As many know, foot caressing and massage is an art that is simultaneously grounding and arousing. If your partner seems a little "spacy"—that is, not fully present in his or her body— and not as responsive as usual to caresses, a foot massage may be just what's needed. The feet (and the ears as well) provide access to all the internal organs through the body meridians. Thus, massaging the feet gives your partner's physical and subtle body a complete energy workout!

Light caressing of the face—particularly the eyes, lips, and ears—is invariably a deeply intimate experience for both partners. Perhaps because the face is so familiar visually, caressing it brings out surprisingly tender feelings of love. Some time ago we realized that we had been neglecting each other's faces in our caressing. The discovery was made during a pre-lovemaking council when Jaquelyn responded to Jack's question about the kind of touching she preferred before penetration:

"I like kissing—deep and sweet. I like to be held and stroked. I like to feel the energy move along my spine. I like a lot of this before breasts and genitals get involved. First the back, spine, and shoulders; then the face, lightly touched. I like to be told that I'm loved and beautiful. Then kissing. When this all unfolds slowly, them I'm ready for everything. My mouth is very sensuous, like a sexual organ. I like sweet talk."

Seven

Interpenetration and the Art of Sexual Communion

Just your look brings him to life
The cobra entranced, rising, teaching me
How to love all over again

Our Kegel conversations are sublime
Undulating poetry in slow motion
That invites the stillness of union

Prancing sweater girl, Yoni sorceress, lotus keeper
Your multicolored mysteries
Rival Eve's at the start of the journey

$\mathcal{D}$uring our early attempts at sexual communion, we held many councils to discuss what we had learned from our explorations. The following is a portion of one of those dialogues.

Jaquelyn: We're riding the wave better and better lately, but I still have the feeling I could entice you into coming if I let myself go completely. My yearning for you to fill me is so strong that if I would pull out all the stops, I think you'd go over the edge.

Jack: That sounds like a delightful challenge...But you're probably right. When you really let the energy flow and get close yourself, I feel like you could pull me over the waterfall.

Jaquelyn: Of course, that's not the game. I have to set a strong intent not to do the natural thing, which is to contract around your cock and make you come. I've also been exploring the spreading surrender movement: setting the intention to expand my field, slowing my breath, spreading my legs wider and wider, and keeping my pelvis still. That's what I do if I feel you're losing your focus and getting too close to the waterfall.

Jack: I've been doing a similar expansion-surrender-breathing movement, too. It brings me right to the crest of the wave, but if you're in spreading surrender at the same time, I won't go over the edge.

Jaquelyn: Yes, as long as you stay conscious. Remember, I want you to be present in *me*, not lost in your own sensations. Imagining the energy moving upward and downward from my yoni plus deep exhaling also help me if climax comes too close. It also helps me to remember our intention *not* to come. All this takes practice, but the practice is such fun!

Jack: Telling you what images I'm having helps me to keep my balance, too, although sometimes our talking turns up the heat.

Jaquelyn: Even if I don't move very much, I bet talking seductively or those little groans of pleasure would push you over the edge.

Jack: Maybe I could seduce you with a lot of sweet, sexy talk...

Jaquelyn: Promises, promises!

Jack: Let's face it. My cock has a mind of its own. But when we interpenetrate—when our subtle bodies are both entering and receiving each other simultaneously—the spreading surrender grows naturally. Then I feel the boundary between our genitals disappearing. All I'm aware of is that incredible bridge between our sexual chakras.

Jaquelyn: That's been our primary energy connection, for sure. But if we image the heart and mind bridges, too, we could go even further. Imagining all three bridges while we're interpenetrating helps me to keep expanding.

Jack: It's amazing how our imaginal weaving shapes the whole pattern of arousal now more than our ordinary minds. All this depends on trust, of course—my trusting you to be true to our intent not to come and being able to restrain any unconscious desire you might have to feel more powerful than I. I suppose you have to trust me the same way. A lot of men don't feel they're successful lovers unless they get their partner to come.

Jaquelyn: It's the same for women at times, too.

Jack: That kind of imprinting is so strong. We have to get past all that gender and power stuff to carry out this practice.

Jaquelyn: If a lot of people practiced sexual communion, the gender war would end in no time!

☿ Interpenetration

The accessibility of Third Presence in a transcending relationship depends, to a great extent, on the strength of the couple's sexual practices. As in all other aspects of the relationship, these must be of a transcending nature, too. Access to the Imaginal

Realm and becoming aware of the interpenetration of the couple's subtle bodies are the keys to Third Presence. The same keys unlock the secrets of sexual communion.

The heart of sexual communion is the practice of interpenetration. This balanced interaction of the couple's physical and subtle bodies is a multidimensional form of lovemaking that embraces ordinary conscious-ness and the Imaginal Realm at the same time. The partners go be-yond what they have already explored in the world of secular sexuality by becoming equally aware of the interaction of their energy fields. During sexual communion, they are in an expanded state of consciousness in which they are aware of visionary images as well as the workings of the ordinary mind. This state offers the lovers many gifts, including the ability to witness their emotional interactions with greater detachment.

The Third is close at hand during interpenetration because of the emphasis on the interweaving of the subtle bodies. This interweaving opens partners to the ecstatic union that we have come to associate with the grace of the Divine Pair. During inter-penetration, partners have an opportunity to experience the Divine Pair in themselves.

The challenge of sexual communion is to transcend the pat-terns of secular sexuality in four major areas: movement, imaging, perception, and communication. Rather than the familiar vigorous and large-scale movements, *subtle movements and stillness* predomi-nate; *visionary imagination* enhances the thoughts and patterns of the ordinary mind; *the ability to "see" subtle bodies* in the etheric domain complements normal vision; and ordinary communication is expanded by more *intuitive interactions* that ultimately become nonverbal.

In this chapter we explore ways to support these transitions and open lovemaking to Third Presence and a glimpse of the Divine Pair. The primary challenge is to go beyond the usual patterns of orgasmic discharge—physically, emotionally, and mentally. A brief history of traditional practices for accomplishing this, most of which relates to the withholding of ejaculation by the male, is provided in Appendix 2. However, we are interested in balanced practices in which the man and woman both share in the exploration of "living on the edge."

When intercourse is experienced primarily in the physical world, the natural roles are *man as penetrator* and *woman as receiver*. This pattern has dominated our sexual lives and influenced much of what happens between the genders. When intercourse is celebrated on both the physical and energetic levels, however, this pattern is altered radically. Using their visionary imaginations, partners can experience the woman's subtle body penetrating the man's at the same time he enters her physically. Making love in both worlds at the same time is the essence of interpenetration.

When this happens with some consistancy, partners soon find themselves interpenetrating in other parts of their mental landscape as well as in the sexual. This leads eventually to their ordinary and visionary levels of consciousness beginning to interpenetrate more generally. The more expansive this interpenetration, the more fully the partners enter into Third Presence and the grace of the Divine Pair.

We are not suggesting that couples set a uniform intention to avoid discharging during sexual intercourse. (Of course, that is always a possibility if they so choose.) We do urge couples to explore the practices of sexual communion so that they *have the choice* either to stay on the edge or *consciously* to embrace the orgasmic experience when they feel that alternative is desirable.

Movement and Stillness

During interpenetration, the partners' joint visionary imagination is empowered, in part, through the flow of energy along the penis-vagina bridge that connects their sexual chakras. (See the accompanying illustration.)

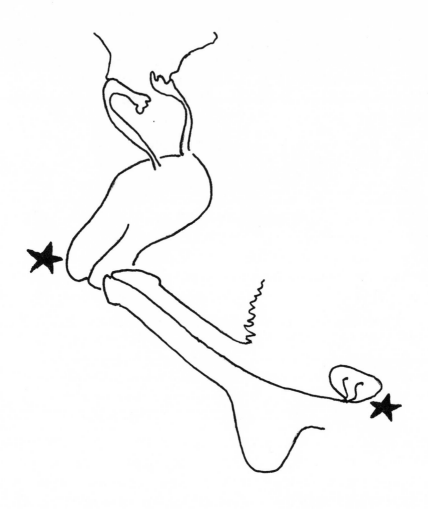

The midpoint of this bridge is the woman's G-spot, which is located on the ventral wall of the vagina between the cervix and the vaginal opening.[1] This thickened, vascular area is capable of responding to both direct physical stimulation and focused awareness. The flow of energy in both directions across the genital

[1] See also Chapter 2.

bridge requires very little friction to be maintained and, in fact, can take place in a state of complete stillness. The strong rhythmic motion we associate with climax-directed intercourse is unnecessary during the practice of interpenetration. *The movement of energy and the co-creative use of visionary imagination—not large-scale physical movement— are the primary catalysts for arousal and pleasure in sexual communion.*

To arrive at this realization usually takes a lot of experimenting because most of us are used to associating good sex with the motion-induced friction that leads to climax. For example, when either partner feels the man's erection waning, the usual instinct is to move more vigorously to revive him. However, during interpenetration, fluctuations in the man's erection are natural and, in fact, constitute an integral part of the practice. Automatic intensification of movement when signs of physical arousal wane inhibits the refinements of sexual communion.

Instead the partners can use their visionary imaginations to adjust the level of sexual arousal. For example, they might image the flow increasing across the genital bridge in conjunction with slow and limited physical movement. With time, even micro-movements of the penis and vagina ("micro-Kegels"), using the pubococcygeal muscles that control the pubic floor, are sufficient to maintain and expand the level of arousal.

These movements occur instinctively in some couples, but an intentional micro-Kegel practice can also be acquired. The male organ does not need to be fully erect for this to happen. Ultimately, when the couple's visionary imagination is sufficiently heightened, a state of absolute stillness can be enjoyed in which waves of energy pass through the partners' interpenetrating physical and subtle bodies, each one bringing them more fully into the expanded awareness of Third Presence.[2]

---

[2] A similar state is depicted vividly in the film *Cocoon*.

Practices for Orgasmic Control

As we have emphasized, the greater challenge for most couples is not arousal but rather counteracting the strong movement towards orgasmic climax. Each time the couple make love, there are basically three choices: (1) allow orgasm-discharge without restraint, (2) postpone the climax until both partners decide they are ready, or (3) move beyond discharge completely. Unlike most traditional practices of ejaculation-spasm control, which focus primarily on the man, we believe both partners are equally responsible for making these decisions and choreographing the dance of interpenetration.

It is usually easier for women than men to allow the degree of surrender that counteracts the urge to orgasm-discharge. This is especially true for women who enjoy deep penetration and have not become attached to rapid and vigorous clitoral stimulation. For most women, the surrender is easier when the woman is lying with her legs spread—for example, in the familiar face-to-face ("missionary") intercourse position. Then, when climax approaches, moving her knees just a little further outward— together with imaging herself spreading wider, perhaps as a flower opening in the sun—allows the sexual energy to spread throughout the body and so avert the climax. This spreading-opening movement also serves to reduce the friction between the vaginal walls and the penis, thus helping the man avoid climaxing.

When first experimenting with this practice of *spreading surrender* in the face-to-face position, it is usually preferable for the partner with the better discharge control to be on top. For many couples this means the man will have the opportunity to be in the bottom position, perhaps exploring the less familiar feelings of vulnerability and surrender that accompany this position. The spreading position may also be physically challenging for some men, which may inspire stretching exercises or yoga to allow the legs to open wider without discomfort. The reversal of position can stimulate a re-evaluation of gender identification, since there is a greater feeling of being penetrated and thus a different kind of vulnerability in the bottom position than the familiar "performance vulnerability" felt by the partner on top. In sexual communion both kinds of vulnerability are shared by the man and woman to an increasing extent as they go deeper into the interpenetrating nature of the practice.

Obviously it takes more restraint for either partner to resist discharge if the other moves with rhythmic abandon. But the real challenge of transformational sexuality is to develop an awareness of more subtle body movements. For example, when the woman contracts her pubococcygeal muscles around the penis, an aware partner will have the sensation that his organ is being physically and energetically massaged or "milked" by the vagina. Similarly, by flexing his pubococcygeal muscles in a pulsing rhythm, the man can move his erect penis up and down, simultaneously stimulating his own blood flow and his partner's vaginal walls or cervix without recourse to the usual thrusting motion.

Clear communication is another ally in prolonging and expanding interpenetration. To begin with, it is wise to communicate simply and directly ("I'm getting close," "Go slow," or just "Whoa!"). Eventually each partner will learn to detect when the other's climax is approaching, physiologically and energetically, thereby permitting continual adjustments in muscle activity, movement, and imaging.

Positions in Lovemaking

In the face-to-face position the partner on top generally has to maintain at least a modest amount of large muscle control. Any resulting physical strain can increase the desire to release body tension by climaxing. Since sexual communion requires that both partners are comfortable enough to sustain interpenetration for extended periods (half an hour to an hour at least), the couple need to experiment with a variety of positions until they find one or more in which this can be accomplished.

An arrangement that works for most couples is the *scissors position*, which is particularly good for partners of markedly different size, since each person supports almost all his or her own weight in this configuration.[3] To assume the scissors position, partners lie side by side, the lighter one (say, the woman) lying on her back and the man lying on his side turned towards her. She lifts and opens her legs slightly and the man places his lower leg under the woman's leg that is closer to him. The man's top leg is placed between the woman's legs as she turns slightly towards him. Then they adjust their bodies until their genitals meet comfortably. The man need not have a large erection for this practice and can even be "stuffed" (inserted into the vagina manually) before becoming erect in order to initiate interpenetration.

In the scissors both partners' hands are free for caressing, although kissing is not as convenient as in the missionary position. Most important, refined and relaxed movements are easily maintained in the scissors position and, after some practice, contractions of the partners' pubococcygeal muscles are usually sufficient to maintain arousal. The sense of weightlessness and comfort in this position facilitates the breathing and imagery necessary to stay on the edge of climax and so sustain subtle body interpenetration for longer periods.

We should also mention the classical tantric position (depicted in the "Yab-Yum" or sacred marriage tankas), although most couples find this configuration impossible or at least uncomfortable to maintain for more than a few moments.[4] Sitting in a full or partial lotus position is difficult enough for most men without the additional challenge of carrying the full weight of a partner. However, by adapting this position slightly, it can be made available to more couples. The man (or whoever is heavier) sits in a comfortable straight-back chair or on the edge of a bed. The

---

[3] For an excellent and detailed description of this position, see *The Art of Sexual Ecstasy*, Margo Anand, J.P. Tarcher, 1989.
[4] The Yab-Yum (literally father-mother) tankas depict the sacred marriage of compassion and emptiness in the Mahayana path or skillful means and wisdom in the Vajra path.

woman straddles the man, sitting on his lap with her legs wrapped around his lower waist and hips. Interpenetration of the genitals is then readily accomplished, hands are free for caressing, and the couple can easily explore kissing and energy exchanges such as eye resonance. Other advantages of this traditional position include aligned vertical spines (which encourages movement of energy in the subtle bodies) and the resulting proximity of the partners' chakras. The main challenges of the configuration are maintenance of the sitting position without back strain to either partner and the requirement for the man to carry the woman's entire weight on his upper thighs.

The Intermingling of Subtle Bodies

As interpenetration is maintained and the urge to discharge transmuted into deeper surrender, the partners' sexual energy grows beyond a focus on their sexual chakras, spreading throughout their physical and subtle bodies, ascending their spinal columns, and heightening awareness of the other centers. The throat chakra plays an important role in this expansion, since it enjoys a special energetic link with the sexual center. Recall from our discussion in Chapter 4 that the throat is associated with the intuitive and image-making capabilities that are central to artistic creation. Hand-scans of the etheric field reveal a well-defined channel between the sexual and throat centers through which the energy flow can be readily stimulated in both directions. During sustained interpenetration, the sexual-throat channel provides the route for further opening of the throat center, thus empowering the creative imaging and intuition needed in the practice. This sexual-throat channel, which has long been familiar to people sensitive to the energetic level, is a primary reason why heightened sexual arousal and visionary imagination are so profoundly connected.

For many people the awakening of visionary imagination during sexual communion produces a harvest of sensory images associated either with the heart center, the brow, or sometimes both in rapid succession. One partner's awakening can ignite the other, further heightening the shared state of erotic love. Sometimes the climactic rush of the heart union is so strong that the temptation is to "go out" of the mind in a way that is analogous to the physiological experience just before orgasmic discharge. If either partner loses consciousness in this way, one or both may be drawn into physical climax. Maintaining awareness during heart union is aided by becoming a *fully present witness* of the entire experience. The commitment to simultaneously witness and participate in the merging of heart centers helps to maintain the couple on the edge of physical discharge and expands the loving state of subtle body interactions still further.

Witness presence can be strengthened through a pattern of relaxed breathing that includes a slow and complete exhalation cycle. Keeping the eyes open and focusing attentively on one's partner also helps to avoid drifting into a private reality. These simple practices permit witnessing energetic and physical sensations around the heart and elsewhere in a relatively objective way. The result is an increase in the partners' recognition and appreciation of their love for each other. Thus witnessing actually increases the heart union, which in turn increases the energy flow between the partners' subtle bodies. This state can be prolonged indefinitely if the partners remain awake, expand, and surrender in a way that is analogous to the practice of delaying genital orgasm.

Sustaining the heart union increases erotic feelings in other subtle body centers as well. A heightening in the solar plexus may be felt next, although this center is so active under normal circumstances that most people only notice large shifts in energy. As the flow moves up the spine, partners may become aware of the opening and union of their brow centers (if this has not already happened simultaneously with the heart), evidenced by a burst of sensory imagery. The union of the crown centers is usually the last to make its presence known, since direct detection of this chakra generally requires greater sensitivity. When the lovers are able to witness the simultaneous awakening of their energy centers, they enter the ecstatic state of visionary imagination and physical pleasure that is the harvest of sexual communion practice.

Y

A Council During Interpenetration– Later in the Journey

Several years ago, as part of our research and exploration, we decided to tape a dyadic council on sexual communion while we were actually making love. The intention was to see what additional insights about the practice would arise in this heightened state of visionary imagination. The following is a "slightly edited" version of our dialogue.

Jack: I'm in you and in my mind, too, but it's difficult to stay present in both at the same time. Talking brings in analytical thinking and my sense of contact with my body and the Imaginal Realm diminishes.

Jaquelyn: Imagine we're in all those places at the same time.

Jack: I used to think that making love and being in my mind were incompatible. My excuse for getting lost in body sensations was the need to get out of my head. You called it "going unconscious." It's different now. I wonder if my mind is getting eroticized.

Jaquelyn: If your mind is fully erotic, you can be mentally present and in your body at the same time. The mind needs to have a little fun once in a while!

Jack: My more logical, rational mind and the part that sees the goddess in you are finally merging.

Jaquelyn: At last! If you connect your cock and your mind, images can be transmitted directly. The image of me as goddess will come through your cock and I'll feel it inside me...Does talking like this make you feel like a sexual-spiritual object [*laughter*]?

Jack: Okay, I'll see if I can make the connection...[*pause*]...The old pattern is still strong. I feel like I'm trying to change my basic circuitry.

Jaquelyn: Remember the image of the energy bridge joining our sexual centers. See your cock getting harder as the flow increases. Take the image all the way into your body.

Jack: Okay, I'll try...[*pause*]...I actually see it!

Jaquelyn: See what?

Jack: A shaft surrounded by a sheath. There's light between my cock and your vagina. There's light in there! I could—

Jaquelyn: —It's my turn to be the director [*laughter*]...Use the light to locate your sexual center. Feel the flow across the bridge into my sexual center.

Jack: I have an image of my center, about two inches back from the base of my cock, deep inside...I can feel yours, too. It's a little beyond and below where I am, near the cervix.

Jaquelyn: Right. If you stop moving completely, the energy will make the leap directly to my center like a spark jumping...[*pause*]...What's happening now?

Jack: I'm bringing my mind into the space between the end of my cock and your sexual center. I usually think of my thoughts being up in my head, not in my body, but now my mind *is* the spark itself.

Jaquelyn: Goody! You'll soon have a sexual mind just like mine!

Jack: [*pause*]...When I'm silent, I can bring my mind all the way into my body. When I talk, it shifts back to where it usually hangs out. It's strange to have a choice.

Jaquelyn: Do you feel how the union of our sexual centers affects our hearts?

Jack: Let me check it out...[*pause*]...My logical mind is rebelling a little at being directed...[*pause*]...Yes, I feel my heart expanding, wave after wave. I know I could get even more aroused physically by ending this dialogue and getting into my body more. But that's the old way and not our intention now...It's still strange to be talking so much while we're making love...[*pause*]...My mind feels like it's being irradiated!

Jaquelyn: If you could make an even stronger connection between your brow and sexual centers, your whole pelvis would be activated. Use me as a lightning rod...You connect to your cock in a new way every time we make love, don't you?

Jack: Yes, through you.

Jaquelyn: See, you use me as a sexual object, too [*laughter*]. But you have a choice now: use your mind as the spark and let it jump to me...What's happening now?

Jack: The floor is getting uncomfortable [*laughter*].

Jaquelyn: That just made me realize how important it is to stay in my body. I wasn't feeling the floor at all.

Jack: Our connection wavered there for a moment and I'm losing my erection. If you'd stay more grounded, I could go out further and we'd be in better balance...There's a certain energy you put out that always gets me hard, but that fades when you disappear too far into the Imaginal Realm. When you're there you seem to lose interest in the physical domain. It feels to me like you wander away and get lost. Maybe that's why you often urge me to join you.

Jaquelyn: I've always thought it was you who got lost, but maybe I do leave first by going out of my body too much.

Jack: I don't think there's a "first." We're doing this together.

Jaquelyn: Maybe you're worrying that you were so deep inside me you'd never see your cock again [*laughter*]!

Jack: Once a Freudian, always a Freudian...Merging the subtle bodies is important, but the erotic connection still has to be physical, too. Visionary imagination also needs grounding on the physical or it drifts away.

Jaquelyn: Okay. Let's see if we can get the energy to flow the other way. I'll penetrate you with my subtle body and you take me in. Imagine the energy moving from your genitals, up your spine, out the top of your head, and then down into me.

Jack: Okay, we know it works well the other way...[*pause*].

Jaquelyn: You're having a hard—I mean soft—time getting out of your head [*laughter*]!

Jack: Hey, this is an experiment. No judgments. I was still imaging reversing the energy in the loop.

Jaquelyn: Oh, I'm sorry...[*pause*].

Jack: Yes, the flow is coming into me and up my spine now.

Jaquelyn: We're interpenetrating!...[*pause*]...To do this I have to completely stop being Mother and just be Priestess. The mother takes in—and produces children. Now instead of taking you in, I'm penetrating you. You're the female.

Jack: We're working with the subtle bodies. We don't need to call anything male or female.

Jaquelyn: Right...[*pause*]...I have to admit a slight preference for taking you in over penetrating, although I have to work harder to stay conscious when the flow is more into me.

Jack: That's what I meant by asking you to be more grounded on the physical level. We have to stay conscious as we surrender. If you go out, it's not really surrendering. That's the way we used to make love in the beginning...For me, both ways are okay. I like being penetrated, but penetrating your subtle body is great too, like this...[*pause*].

Jaquelyn: Delicious...I'm surrendering and staying right here...It's so-o-o delicious...[*pause*].

Jack: We just went through another gateway. The waves of energy are amazing!

Jaquelyn: We stayed pretty conscious, too. Our Third is right here.

Jack: Yes. I'm seeing the Yab-Yum image, like in our tanka, with your legs wrapped around me.

Jaquelyn: The image of sacred marriage.

Jack: Two becoming one...[*long pause*].

Jaquelyn: You were pretty present there, darling. It's a little scary to make such a strong connection between the worlds.

Witnessing the Council

This experiment, other personal adventures, and our work with many couples have led us to a number of general observations.

- Sexual body-mind patterning is deep and tenacious, but it can be changed through the combination of interpenetration and visionary imagination.

- Transcendent lovemaking is grounded in the body. *Sexual communion does not mean leaving the body behind but rather incorporating more and more aspects of nonordinary reality into the physical experience.*

- The combination of visionary imagination and interpenetration can eroticize the mind. Images can be transferred to the body with surprising effectiveness.

- During interpenetration, the subtle bodies are actually making love in the Imaginal Realm. Activating visionary imagination during lovemaking allows the lovers to affect the flow of sexual energy in their subtle bodies and refine their physical responses.

- Surrendering during lovemaking requires staying conscious and is not to be confused with abandoning mind awareness.

- Being in Third Presence during sexual communion does not prevent each partner from recognizing imperfections in the other. Divine blessings and realistic perceptions can coexist on the path of a transcending relationship.

- Visionary imagination during interpenetration inspires humor as well as insight.

- Mind and body are truly inseparable. This is both an esoteric truism and a state of being that is felt with particular clarity during interpenetration.

- There is much for all of us to learn about the mystery of lovemaking. We are just beginning to glimpse what's possible along the path of the heart.

Part 3

The Harvest of Third Presence

Eight

Dynamics of an Awakened Relationship

Holding each other in the morning
Heart to heart, motionless
Breath dissolving boundaries, minds silent
Welcoming our otherworldly ally

All this time a sanctuary has been growing
A hidden grotto discovered, silent, mysterious
A forest shrine found beyond the din of desire
A temple manifesting, stone by stone

Ordinary stones, divine mortar
Divine stones, ordinary mortar

$\mathcal{W}$hat are the tangible benefits of Third Presence? This state of consciousness, whether it includes direct encounters with an otherworldly ally or not, invariably produces a harvest of improvements in the quality of the couple's relationship. In this chapter we will explore a few of the ways in which access to Third Presence nourishes the love and enlightens the dynamics of a transcending relationship.

Stability and Conflict Resolution

Since they are governed by the partners' personalities, the dynamics of a secular relationship tend to be patterned and predictable. Generally, the growth of both individuals and the partnership itself is interrupted frequently by interludes of tension and miscommunication. Equanimity is a fleeting blessing. A secular relationship is like trying to balance oneself on a two-legged stool. The inevitable instabilities make it difficult to build trust.

Another "leg" is needed for balance. In a transcendent relationship the Third's insightful voice provides a stabilizing presence that allows a couple to take the risks necessary for the relationship's continued growth. We can represent the situation graphically by means of the simple relational triangle shown below:

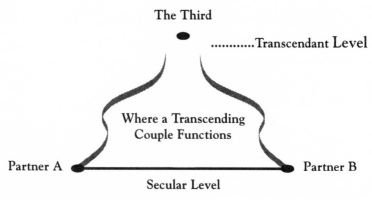

Broadly speaking, the joys and pains of a secular relationship take place as a sequence of interactions (celebrations, conflicts, compromises, agreements) that occur "along the line" joining the two partners—that is, within the restricted dimensions of their ordinary lives. (Many aspects of the agreements and compromises occur unconsciously and would more appropriately be called *arrangements*.) When the two partners are in deep conflict and cannot compromise, there is no alternative but to back off, take a deep breath, and try again. We are all familiar with the feeling of having the same basic argument with our partner again and again in a thousand different ways. Secular partners live primarily in the world created by their personalities. The old teaching, "You can't solve the problem from the level of the problem," comes to mind.

In contrast, when two partners learn to access Third Presence in their relationship, the alternatives for interaction expand beyond the secular level to include a portion of the transcendent domain (as shown in the figure). Transcending partners discover they have ways to get beyond their difficulties other than with-drawing and trying again. They have an "additional dimension" in which to maneuver. The more developed the Third's presence, the greater the room for relating and the more choices they have for handling the challenges. With greater choice comes the trust that a path through the difficulties will be found. With the aid of council and other practices, the partners learn to treat their conflicts as opportunities for learning and growth.

In particular, regular access to Third Presence helps partners to let go of their attachments to strongly held emotional patterns. For example, a couple might go through some or all of the follow-ing steps (not necessarily in this order) as their council dialogue unfolds:

1. I'm angry and justified in my anger.

2. I see that my partner feels the same way.

3. I had better take a deep breath and step back from the fire a little.

4. OK, we're in one of those situations where we need help.

5. What's going on right now? I could defend myself, but I'm actually more interested in what's happening *between us*.

6. We've been in conflicts like this before and learned from them. With a little help, we can increase our understanding of the dynamic between us.

7. We could call another council.

8. We could ask for a dream.

9. We could use the embrace meditation to rebalance our subtle bodies.

10. We could set out the third pillow, enter Third Presence, and listen.

Third Presence and the availability of the practices allow the couple to function more spaciously, unblocking the stalemate and creating the necessary room to negotiate. The more accessible Third Presence is, the less likely partners will stay stuck at the first step. Notice how the witness perspective plays a central role in the movement to step 2 and beyond. The ability to witness what's happening without denying one's feelings is essential in breaking logjams and is one of the hallmarks of a transcending relationship. Another is the humility required in many of the steps from 4 on.

Both *witnessing* and *acknowledging the need for help* are indications that partners can access Third Presence, since they both imply the existence of a source of insight beyond what both partners have to offer. Once the exploratory tone enters in step 5, a path through the conflict usually opens, beginning with the partners' awareness (step 6) that they have weathered such storms before and learned that conflicts are opportunities for each of them and the relationship to grow. The availability of steps 8, 9, and 10 is important. Every conflict need not be resolved verbally, as in step 7. In fact, when partners are acting like a pair of verbal bulldogs, it is often better for them to disengage and move into Third Presence through one of the silent practices.

Mature couples will recognize this as an elaboration of the wisdom of "sleeping on it" when a conflict seems unresolvable. The partners are more likely to be able to let go of their positions if they trust in a continuing presence that has the best interests of the relationship at heart—that is, if they trust their access to Third Presence. The regular practices of a transcending relationship support the building of this trust. For example, sharing dreams, dyadic council, and a variety of energy exchange exercises offer ways to unravel conflicts directly or indirectly, since they all have the capability to moderate the mind's affinity for attachment.

❈

Manifestations of the Third

Once established and supported by the partners' practices, the Third can be experienced in many ways: words of guidance from the third pillow, "heard" by one or both partners during a dyadic council; a glimpse of the relationship's future while walking along a country road at dusk; a time of sublime clarity, early in the morning after sharing a dream; or a vision of the archetypal forces that shape the relationship story during the afterglow of lovemaking.

Most manifestations of the Third occur as co-creations of the couple's visionary imagination. However, the Third can appear to only one of the partners, particularly during times of heightened intensity. The following story suggests how much a transcending relationship has in common with the tradition of the shamanic journey.[1] The scene is the mountains of Central Colorado, in the

[1] We began to collect material for this book many years ago under the working title *Shamanic Relationship*. We soon decided the term would be unnecessarily inaccessible and perhaps misleading. Nevertheless, the spirit of the shamanic tradition has informed much of our exploration of Third Presence. This perspective is elaborated further in Appendix 3.

mid-eighties, during a short summer retreat. Jack tells the story.

Jaquelyn and I had made plans to create a private remarriage ceremony to honor our commitment to further awakening the transcending nature of our relationship. The idea had occurred to us long before we arrived at the isolated cabin that a friend had provided for our retreat. Not surprisingly, preparations for the occasion had stirred up old conflicts that needed further resolution. In particular, Jaquelyn had confronted me with her strong feeling that I had over-accommodated a few of my colleagues at the Ojai Foundation with whom I had been working for several years. "You're diluting yourself again," she said. "Trying to please so many people takes energy away from our relationship and prevents it from going deeper. I wonder if you're afraid."

I defended the importance of the Foundation's work and denied that my intense engagement with the community was a way to avoid intimacy with her. She wasn't reassured and after several hours of trying to resolve this and other issues, we lapsed into silence. I decided to take a walk along the fire road near the cabin in order to let go of my dark mood before the remarriage ceremony planned for that evening.

I had gone only a mile, lost in a cloud of confusion, when I heard the shriek of a large bird behind me. I continued walking without looking up. The second, much louder call penetrated my self-absorption.

At that moment, the sun came out from behind the clouds and the bird's large shadow appeared ahead of me, moving slowly along the road. I stopped and looked up in time to see an imposing female golden eagle land on the tip of a lodgepole pine, only thirty feet from where I was standing. She displayed her beautiful markings by aligning her body perpendicularly to my line of sight and began slowly ruffling her reddish brown-and-white tail feathers. Her dance-like movements lured me into greater attentiveness.

She never looked directly at me but continued ruffling her feathers in a way that felt vaguely erotic. I had the immediate impression she was conveying something important about my relationship with Jaquelyn. I responded by going through the visionary doorway that she had opened. What I "heard" over the next few minutes, standing still in the road, sounded something like this:

"When are you going to stop playing the game of pleasing so many parents—and pouting when you get reprimanded? It's time to get your thumb out of your mouth and be more courageous, particularly in searching for the truth in a difficult situation. Only a mature man can enter the kind of love you and your woman want to share now...Are you ready to commit?" (The last was transmitted with the tone of, "Shit, or get off the pot!")

I found myself accepting the challenge without defensiveness. In the heightened state, the truth of her challenge was self-evident. She became perfectly still and waited for my response. As soon as I nodded, the eagle let out two shrieks and took off towards the sun.

It rained lightly on the way home. As soon as I entered the cabin, Jaquelyn asked me what had happened. "Why do you ask?" I responded.

"You seem different," she said.

Our ceremony was strong that evening and included reaching a new level of surrender in our lovemaking. The next day I placed an offering of raisins and nuts at the foot of the tree where the eagle had landed.

Experiences such as this are often discribed as visions, moments of truth, or epiphanies. However, in time, Third Presence is experienced more as an *ongoing parallel reality* than a spontaneous visitation from spirit. The phenomenological aspect becomes less important and is replaced by a more ongoing state of well-being and trust. A sense of interactive spaciousness develops in the relationship that permits engaging even the darkest and most difficult issues. The partners begin to feel that the triad with the Third can handle whatever might arise. With growing trust, progressively greater risks can be taken, and so the relationship flourishes.

A Temple of the Third

When conflict, doubt, or the urge to separate arise in a relationship, it is difficult to remember the blessings of intimacy. Anger and grief are often the result of shaken trust in one's partner.

Many couples live through these periods, sometimes at the expense of considerable mental and emotional anguish, wondering why relationship has to be so difficult or why the upheavals cannot be understood and embraced with greater equanimity. Such relationships may endure, but the stress of surviving these painful upheavals can leave little time and energy to fuel new growth.

When Third Presence abides in a relationship, the cycles of separation and intimacy can actually temper the love, much as a blacksmith strengthens his work by alternately immersing it in fire and cool water. The key is the continuity provided by a well-established access to Third Presence, even when the connection between the partners is disrupted for a period of time.

We call the abiding nature of a transcending relationship the *Temple of the Third*. The "Temple" is a co-creation of the partners' visionary imagination that manifests the enduring presence of their relationship in the Imaginal Realm. Entering the Temple becomes a way for partners to enter Third Presence. Within its walls, they are more likely to be touched by the grace of the Divine Pair.

The Temple provides a place of celebration in times of joyous intimacy and a place of refuge in times of pain. In making room for both, the Temple reminds us that our lives move in cycles of *consolation* and *desolation*. These cycles have been well-known to individual seekers on the spiritual path. For example, Ignatius of Loyola spoke passionately of certain practices he developed that permit embracing consolation and desolation both as part of the practitioner's relationship to Christ.[2]

In difficult times, the issues challenging the relationship can be brought to the Temple by each partner, alone or together. These become the raw material out of which the structure is solidified and expanded later when reconciliation occurs. Acknowledgment of the abiding Third, doing the practices with devotion, and the inspiration of the Divine Pair are the cohering forces that create the Temple in the Imaginal Realm. When next the partners are consoled—say, by the grace of sexual communion—the reconciliation of their differences strengthens the Temple further.

The Temple can be imagined concretely in many ways: as a clearing in the forest, a stone sanctuary in the mountains, a hut at the beach, a sacred kiva, a sublime cathedral, or simply a room in the couple's home. The partners may agree on the image to manifest or they may each see and speak of the Temple in a somewhat different way. The Temple's imaginal coherence grows slowly, through the power of the partners visionary imaginations, primarily when they are together intimately doing their practices. The image may change over time, as does a garden, but as long as it is tended, the Temple's presence in the Imaginal Realm will be abiding.

After a while the Temple's continued creation and maintenance take on a life of their own. The partners assume different roles in its ongoing creation as intuition and the realities of the

---

[2] *The Spiritual Exercises of St. Ignatius*, translated by Anthony Motella, Image Books, 1964; and *The Autobiography of St. Ignatius of Loyala*, translated by Joseph F. O'Callaghan, Harper Torchbooks, 1974.

relationship direct—being, at different times, creator, priest or priestess, steward, or refugee. When one partner becomes lost and the other reaches out from the Temple, the call is more easily heard, since in that sacred place it is motivated less from personal need than from wanting a playmate and co-worshiper.

Jack wrote the following expression of gratitude for the Temple many years ago at the conclusion of a council with our Third. We had recently emerged from a difficult time in our relationship, during which the Temple served as a place of refuge for us both.

> I am grateful for the shelter our Temple provides when I am troubled and contracted. When old patterns overtake me, I can shed them here. If I am angry because Jaquelyn is unable to take care of my wounds, I can find sanctuary here. If I lose the hope and good humor that stems from knowing that my Beloved and I are eternally interconnected, I can find renewal in this place of spirit.

> Before the Temple was built, when doubt haunted me, I would turn away from Jaquelyn and struggle alone. Now I take refuge here instead of withdrawing. Here I encounter memories of times when the pain of fragmentation was eased and my heart felt free again. Praying here embraces my confusion as a natural part of the larger mystery. In this sanctuary I dare to look into the mirror of truth.

> There are many forms of the Temple and many faces of the Third to be found inside. My hands know the touch of the stones, since I have been a mason here. My eyes know the quality of the light, for I have witnessed it change a thousand times in this place. Once I looked up and saw windows of color set afire by the sun. Sometimes there are no walls at all, only a strong presence, still and resonant, without shape or substance. Whatever its form, entering the Temple is like coming to a secret shrine in nature or like the feeling of our subtle bodies settling into a lover's embrace.

I never fail to receive consolation here for my pain of separation. Coming to know these heart cycles of contraction and expansion is one of the Temple's greatest gifts. Here trust grows again slowly in the silence, until once again I feel whole and at peace. In the Temple, I know that reconciliation will follow in its own time. I find little gifts here left during previous visits: the end of a candle, a photograph, and the lingering presence of my Beloved.

I've come to trust this place as I depend on the dawn, the movement of the seasons, and the magic of the light at the end of day. Although each cycle of nature and the movements of relationship may surprise me, there are rhythms I can trust in both mysteries.

Nine
The Divine Pair

Since the awakening our lovemaking carries us
Beyond worldly landscapes
Into the realm where spirits play
With Sufis worshiping their Beloveds
"Alchemy," we whisper in the soft gold light

We began our exploration of Third Presence by describing the Third as *a construct in the Imaginal Realm that is useful in understanding the expanding nature of consciousness in a transcending relationship.* We saw how couples can enter the Imaginal Realm through their visionary imagination, using a variety of practices that ultimately takes the experience of the Third beyond specific images and constructs, indeed beyond form itself.

We offered the hypothesis that the Third is made up of the interaction of the partners' subtle bodies plus emanations of the Divine Pair. Accepting the first part of this description requires only an appreciation of esoteric anatomy. Since most people can actually detect another person's subtle body through the simple process of hand-scanning, that part of our hypothesis is on firm ground. But how do we deal with the source of the "emanations"?

As we have done with the Third, we can identify the Divine Pair as an Imaginal Realm construct that has proven useful in our exploration of relationship. However, this description falls far short of capturing its numinous quality. The effects of the emanations we have experienced, both in our own relationship and in the Circle of Lovers practice described in Chapter 5, are remarkably tangible and unmistakably real—as well as long-lasting.

When friends, clients, or the remnants of our own skeptical minds say, "The Divine Pair—and the Third for that matter—are only creations of your imagination," we usually begin by picking up on the word *only*. Its use exposes the ordinary mind's view that the physical world is more real—and, therefore, more important—than the Imaginal Realm. But the power of visionary imagination in a transcending relationship leaves no doubt that these two worlds are equally real and abundantly interconnected.

Besides, we remind the skeptic, images shape how we relate, whether we are conscious of them or not. Cultural stereotypes and imprints from the families of origin strongly affect our relationships, particularly in their early stages and during periods of vulnerability and stress. Even if we are unaware of their existence, these imprints influence how every one of us falls in love, relates to our partner, and creates a family. Why not attempt to create more productive images consciously?

∽

The Evolution of Divinity

Along the transcending path, couples feel a strong invitation to use their visionary imagination to *co-create new images and models for their intimate relationships that are independent of the ones originally imprinted by the culture and families of origin.* This "call" leads to two intriguing questions: What if a composite Divine Pair archetype actually exists in the Imaginal Realm—as have other entities that have long inspired humankind's spiritual passions? What if this manifestation of the Ultimate Mystery has always existed and is now ready to be widely recognized?

More explicitly, let us consider the possibility that *the Divine Pair is a transcultural archetype carrying an aspect of the Ultimate Mystery that is urgently needed now for the further evolution of the human condition.* To begin, we offer first a few historical reflections mixed with personal experience.

The Need for a Divine Pair

Although the couple and the nuclear family are relatively new in human history as societal entities, they have been consistently supported by our traditional religious and cultural values over the past several hundred years. Furthermore, dreamwork and exploratory processes such as age regression suggest that in our primordial and preverbal unconscious memory, each of us carries the instinctual knowledge of belonging to a male-female dyad.[1] As we grow into adulthood, our emerging sexual drive moves most of us inexorably towards joining with another, at least for short periods of time. In the face of significant instabilities in the institution of marriage, the vast majority of us still doggedly chooses the path of partnership during the greater part of our adult lives. After all, for many creatures, pairing is necessary for the propagation of life.

Yet on a practical level, our skills in relating remain limited. Obviously, something has been missing in our culture's collective vision of relationship, something inspirational and transcendent that is powerful enough to overcome the growing cynicism about the possibility that erotic partnerships can long endure. What are we lacking?

----

[1] Recall the myth that began Chapter 3.

As fundamental as pairing may be to our biological make-up and secular values, for most of us it is no where to be found among the deities that shape our spiritual lives. The primary deities of the world's active religions are solitary males. In moving away from pantheism, the Judaic revelation of the One God has made it challenging to hold a vision of "twoness" as divine (although in mystical Judaism, the Shekina, the feminine face of God, is seen as a primary partner of the Ultimate Divinity). The historical figure-head of Christianity (as well as Islam and, to a lesser extent, Buddhism) expresses the Oneness of God through a single male avatar. The Holy Trinity in Christianity does acknowledge the mysterious multiplicity of the divine, but traditionally all three "parts" of the trinity are male and the only relationship that is honored is the parental one (father-son). (The relatively recent elevation of Mother Mary to quasi-divine status is similarly paren-tal.) There are no lovers with whom we can identify in traditional Christian theology.

Obviously, then, one of the major reasons for the absence of a Divine Pair in our theology is the lack of the presence of an empowered female deity. Having experienced the personal mother as the all-powerful provider of nourishment and the literal source of life as an infant, most of us would naturally embrace a female deity as we grew up—if one were available. At some point many of us have wondered how there could be a "Father God" without a "Mother God." Recent progress (changes in liturgical practice, reawakening of interest in the Goddess, beginning prayers with "Father/Mother God," etc.) is beginning to change the patriarchal deity pattern. Still, most of us live with much of the theological gender imbalance that major spiritual traditions have supported for millennia.

As we traveled the path of transcending relationship, it be-came clear that a Divine Pair had a natural role to play in inspir-ing the spiritual life of our partnership. At one moment, when the love between us was unusually heightened, we saw the Divine Pair as two equally empowered lover deities who constellate ideal relationship for the world's vast array of neophyte couples. Once envisioned, the presence of this pair took hold in our imaginal life and dreams as well.

At first, we treated these images and dreams skeptically as personal projections, partly because of the deep imprinting from Western theology and partly because we had not yet reached a level of comfort with the reality of the Imaginal Realm. But as the images of the Divine Pair persisted and grew stronger, we became convinced that they had a source, *not primarily of our own creation,* that was being made known to us artfully, step by step, as if by a highly intuitive master teacher.

We were further encouraged by our readings. For example, the Tibetan mystic, Lama Govinda, writes[2]:

> The subjectivity of inner vision does not diminish its reality-value. Such visions are not hallucinations, because their reality is that of the human psyche. They are symbols, in which the highest knowledge and the noblest endeavor of the human mind are embodied. Their visualization is the creative process of spiritual projection [his term for visionary imagination], through which inner experience is translated into visible form, comparable to the creative act of an artist whose subjective idea, emotion, or vision is transformed into an objective work of art, which now takes on a reality of its own independent of its creator.

As the reality of a Divine Pair became more tangible in our life together, we realized that its ancestors in Western and Eastern mythology had made relatively little impact on us.[3] We soon arrived at a simple explanation. *The compelling nature of the Divine Couple is the result of this particular moment in history rather than being derived from previous myths and images.* Because of the growing empowerment of women in our culture and the awakening of men, there are a sufficient number of erotic relationships that are

---

[2] *Foundations of Tibetan Mysticism*, Lama Anagarika Govinda, Samuel Weiser, 1973, p. 92.
[3] A few of our thoughts on the matter are summarized in Appendix 4.

conscious enough to "imagine" (become aware of) a pair of divine lovers. We came to believe that *a transcultural theology of erotic relationship is being born.*

Others share this notion. For example, in 1981 the visionary cultural historian William Irwin Thompson argued convincingly that our culture has reached a stage of rapid transition by showing that the "artists" of our era are no longer describing a world that exists but, rather, creating a distinctly new one.[4] Thompson believes, along with such radical theologians as Matthew Fox,[5] that in the epoch about to begin, a sacrament of Eros rather than one of death and crucifixion, will create the consciousness needed in our worldly lives together. Thompson sees the sacrament of Eros as a fully physical sexuality in which the "lovers of eternity" give birth to the world on the physical plane. As mentioned earlier, he suggests that *the spiritual focus of the next cycle will be the male and female together, rather than the solitary male of the past.*

What might all this mean to an individual couple, moving doggedly but devotedly along the path of transcending relationship?

Creating Your Own Image of the Divine Pair

Images of the Divine Pair arose spontaneously through our joint visionary imaginations as a result of carrying out the practices we have described. We presumed that other couples would also encounter this presence in the Imaginal Realm when their visionary imaginations were similarly activated—say, in lovemaking, dreamsharing, energy interactions, and councils. In addition, this joint imaginative process might be stimulated more intentionally through a contemporary form of "deity yoga," a well-known practice of Tibetan Buddhism that came to our attention

---

[4] *The Time Falling Bodies Take to Light: Mythology, Sexuality, and the Origins of Culture,* William Irwin Thompson, St. Martin's Press, 1981.
[5] *The Coming of the Cosmic Christ: The Healing of Mother Earth and the Birth of a Global Renaissance,* Matthew Fox, Harper & Row, 1988.

during our search for lover deities.[6] In deity yoga, the practitioner visualizes him- or herself with the body and qualities of the chosen deity (in the traditional Tibetan context, any one of many forms of the Buddha or their consorts). In an analogous way, we feel a couple can activate their own unique vision of the Divine Pair by using their visionary imagination, for example during sexual intimacy.

In this practice, the woman identifies herself with the "Divine Female Lover," allowing herself to be shown those qualities that would help her move along the transcending path with her partner. Similarly for the man. At the same time, the partners together open themselves to the guidance that will enhance the presence of the Divine Pair in their relationship at that juncture of their journey. These teachings are received in Third Presence and can be renewed regularly. Thus the practice evolves dynamically along with the relationship.

At first (and, perhaps, for some time to come) images of the Divine Pair will probably be influenced by each couple's particular relational experiences and so be of transitional importance as representations of an archetype. However, as it becomes more inspired, visionary imagination transcends relationship particulars and more collective images emerge—if, in fact, an omnipresent archetype is ready to be recognized. Eventually, a Divine Pair "with a thousand faces" might manifest in the Imaginal Realm (analogous to Joseph Campbell's vision of the archetype of the mythological hero).[7] This dual deity would be accessible to the joint consciousness of an inspired couple who *see* with a free and erotically empowered imagination. It is conceivable that this collective perception would eventually transcend not only the diversity of individual relationships but also cultural differences as well.

---

[6] See, for example, *The Tantric Distinction: An Introduction to Tibetan Buddhism*, Jeffrey Hopkins, Wisdom Publications, 1984. An excellent, more recent discussion of deity yoga can be found in *The Tibetan Book of Living and Dying*, Sogyal Rinpoche, Harper San Francisco, 1992.
[7] *The Hero With a Thousand Faces*, Joseph Campbell, Princeton University Press, 1949.

Our current experience teaches us that, as yet, the Divine Pair enjoys only fragments of a mythology. We lack a coherent collection of relationship myths to which lovers can relate the story of their own unique relationship. However, some people believe that the time has come to practice conscious myth-making to achieve our own redemption.[8] We have committed ourselves and our work with other couples to exploring conscious myth-making in partnership. We invite others on the path of intimate love to create images, stories, and other forms of sacred art that celebrate the indwelling deity-guides of their relationships.

A Meditation on the Divine Lovers

As a means for couples to discover their own partnership deities, we offer a guided meditation that is a form of deity yoga, in which the image of the deity is being created or discovered as part of the practice (rather than taken explicitly from a pre-existing tradition). Whether authentic images emerge or not, the meditation should expand the partners' awareness of the inseparability of sexuality and spirituality in their transcending relationship.

One of the partners can record the guiding narrative in a slowed- down, relaxed voice, incorporating appropriate pauses throughout. Then both partners can take the journey together listening to the tape. Alternatively, a recording of the guided meditation is available from the authors that also includes an expanded version of the following instructions.

Preliminary Instructions

It is preferable to do this meditation-visualization when you don't have to rush. You might want to set aside an evening now and then to have a clearing council before the meditation and be prepared for sleep afterwards. Alternatively, if the day's schedule

---

[8] See, for example, *The Mythic Imagination: Your Quest for Meaning through Personal Mythology*, Stephen Larsen, Bantam Doubleday Dell, 1990.

permits, the meditation can be done early in the morning when you may be more rested. We recommend that you listen a number of times; the benefits of the tape grow with repeated listening. Effects are subtle and do not have to be understood with the ordinary mind.

Prior to doing the meditation, it would be good to spend time with each other for a while, perhaps quietly listening to music or taking a leisurely walk. Being rested helps. If you are too tired or distracted, you may drift off somewhere along the way and have little conscious memory of your experience. The guided meditation will still help you, even if you fall asleep, but we recommend doing the practice when you feel rested and peaceful for maximum benefit.

Those familiar with individual meditation may be tempted to enter a familiar solitary state of awareness during the exercise. However, the intention is for the *two of you* to reach these levels *together*. The key to maintaining full consciousness throughout the meditation is to focus on your partner as well as yourself and generally give your attention to more than one aspect of the experience at a time. The exercise is specifically designed to help you develop this capability.

Be sure that you will not be disturbed for at least half an hour and that the temperature of the room is comfortable. It is important to be relaxed and touching each other during this practice. If you want to combine this guided meditation with lovemaking, the scissors position will probably be the most comfortable. You can also hold each other in the embrace meditation, spoon position, or any position where you feel close, relaxed, and are touching— even just gently holding hands.

Guided Meditation

With eyes unfocused or closed, begin to observe your breath. Breathe very softly, slowly, deeply, and quietly. Try to let go of all thoughts and images while watching your breath.

Let everything go now except for watching your breath. Notice how good it feels to slow down and deeply relax.

Now slowly become aware of your partner's breathing, as both of you continue to get quieter and quieter.

Experience the warmth and dearness of your beloved's body. Become aware of the combined scent of your bodies and enjoy their familiarity. Feel the pleasure of your body boundaries making contact with each other. Let yourself feel the full magnetism that occurs between the two of you when you deeply relax together like this.

Breathe between the boundaries wherever your bodies are touching, letting this sensation intensify and then spread throughout your whole being.

As you get quieter and quieter, start to become aware of your own heartbeat. Feel how your heartbeat gently rocks you.

Gradually become aware of your partner's heartbeat, too. It may be hard to tell the difference between the two beats.

Start becoming aware of each other at the chest level. Feel energy flowing between your hearts. The energy may feel so palpable that it seems like an actual presence between you. Imagine this flowing connection to be the *Love Temple* of your relationship. Enjoy the sweetness of being in this Temple. Know that you can always come back to this place for solace and replenishment anytime, wherever you may be.

Whether your genitals are actually touching your lover's right now or not, start tuning into your own sexual feelings. You may initiate this by visualizing your own genitals alternately with visualizing your lover's body and genitals. Even if they are not touching, visualize them in close contact.

For the woman: Very lightly, contract the muscles around and in your vagina. See in your mind's eye small droplets of lubrication beginning to form on your vaginal walls and around your labia. The droplets are crystal clear, even becoming luminous as you watch them. You see your labia swelling a little and becoming very shiny. Remembering how satiny, silky-slick, and slippery your inner juices are, allow yourself to appreciate their warm deliciousness. Feel their radiant magic and enjoy their important role in magnetizing and embracing the entry of your partner's love organ into your inner Love Body. Visualize your mysterious deep genital inner sanctum and see the glowing light just beyond the deepest part of your vagina that emanates from your sexual chakra.

For the man: See now in your mind's eye your penis starting to become warm and slowly enlarging. Use your imagination to go inside it and see the channels opening, welcoming the blood that engorges it until it starts to get firm. See it become darker from the blood as it gets larger and feel it become warmer as you watch it enlarge more and more in your mind's eye. See a tiny clear droplet forming at the urethral opening and imagine it becoming a long silky strand of pure light when you touch it and slowly move your hand away. Feel the pleasure of knowing your love organ can always be prepared to enter your beloved's waiting and ready inner sanctum when you both want that. See the glowing light in your pelvis near your prostate gland that radiates from your sexual chakra.

Both of you feel the sexual energy in your genitals start to spread out all over and through your body.

Now be aware of how your sexual energy interweaves with your partner's. Embrace this combined flow, but don't let it become a desire to act-out in sexual activity. Stay very still. Just open to the flow of energy, perhaps with a few breaths that incorporate long slow exhales. Again, keep feeling the current of energy spread out from your genitals all through your bodies. Be receptive, allowing yourselves to enjoy the deliciousness of receiving without any contraction, body movement, or any need to move into physical activity. Just relax and let the energy flow through you. Relax...relax...relax.

Concentrate now on the flow between your open sexual centers. As you feel this flow going both ways, it becomes the *Erotic Temple* of your relationship...Tune in again to the flow between your two heart centers that we called the Love Temple of your relationship.

Now give your attention to the flow between your sexual chakras and your heart chakras simultaneously. Let yourself start to feel a circular flow between the two of you, joining sexual centers and heart centers at the same time. Let the energy flow in both directions.

Allow yourself to relax more and more into this circular flow until your bodies start feeling porous all over. There is a delicious feeling throughout all your cells, organs, energy centers, and especially your skin where the two of you are touching each other. You're aware of yourselves right now being truly a pair of Love Bodies.

Become aware that your etheric fields are interpenetrating. Feel this combined energy field within and between you creating an expanded consciousness we call Third Presence. This state of awareness is the *High Temple* of your relationship. It contains both your Erotic and Love Temples as well as emanations from a Mystery that is more available to you now. You are in the Imaginal Realm. Your visionary imagination can start creating images now that are sexual, loving, and meditative in building a powerful bridge to Third Presence...[pause]

All your boundaries seem to disappear as you surrender into merging with each other. You may feel yourself start to lose consciousness or awareness of your partner. Stay here; be here right now by focusing on your connection to your partner rather than on your own internal solitary state. You may want to keep your eyes open now. This exercise requires strong discipline at first to stay present. Focus your attention on a mental picture of your interpenetrating genitals to help you stay grounded in your body. The challenge is to stay in a state of body arousal without moving into a desire to act-out. Maintain awareness of both the Erotic and Love Temples in your bodies continually by focusing on your heart and sexual connections and the love you feel for your partner.

In the Imaginal Realm we can glimpse a manifestation of the luminous Divine Pair or Divine Lovers, a dual-entity being that is the archetypal composite of loving couples all over the world from all times. This partnership deity emanates its presence into the Imaginal Realm and inspires all committed relationships.

Now start to visualize an image in your mind's eye of the Divine Lovers. Create in your imagination a vision of an ideal and resplendent partnership that holds all the honesty, beauty, and joy you would like to have in your relationship. See them as a model for how to bring together all the darkness and light in your relationship. They are embracing now just as you are embracing. See them as a highly developed, wondrous image of your authentic selves. See them merging into one another and then moving back into two beings. See the colors and lights shift and dance through them and around them as they move from two into one and back into two again. If seeing the Divine Lovers in human form does not seem natural, you might use colors, moving shapes, and energy flows to create your own representation of Divine Relationship.

See the inspiring creativity of their relationship in the ever-moving lights around them, shimmering and dancing and sustaining them in an eternally changing ecstatic union. Allow yourself to become totally immersed in this vision.

Now bring your attention back to the physical connection with your partner. Hold the vision of the Divine Lovers in your mind's eye while at the same time being fully aware of your physical connection. At first you may want to focus on one and then the other, going back and forth until you learn gradually to focus on both simultaneously…[pause]

Now, as you maintain awareness of your physical connection with your partner, see in your mind's eye that the Divine Lovers are slowly starting to move toward you.

Their image comes closer and closer until you start to sense both of you getting ready to merge with them…You become aware of a heightened energy in your mate as you see her/him fuse with her/his counterpart in the Divine Pair…Feel your own energy become shimmering light all through your body as you merge also…The woman love-partner has become the Divine Lover-Woman…The man love-partner has become the Divine Lover-Man…[pause]

You are fully aware of your own radiance now as well as the luminous field surrounding you and your loved one. It is irresistible to begin to feel at one with your partner as the two of you fuse with the Divine Lovers.

You are aware of feeling at one with your lover as well as your counterpart in the Divine Pair now. Breathe with the energy flows and, with your partner, become one with them. Allow them to flow all through you, feeling an even deeper surrender until you realize that the two of you are already and always have been a manifestation of the Divine Lovers.

Totally relax into this union now beyond images, beyond thoughts. Feel yourselves become pure love relationship. Resting into this love, go into a deep peace and joy, staying there now as long as you like.

ᘐ

Sacred Marriage

Many traditional cultures embrace a vision of sacred marriage as an integral part of spiritual life. For example, at the start of the Lakota pipe ceremony, the joining together of the stem and bowl is seen as the sacred marriage of masculine and feminine principles in nature and ultimately the joining together of heaven and earth. Here the ecstatic union of man and woman arises implicitly in the ceremony.

In contrast, many of the temple images in various forms of Tibetan Buddhism (for example, the Yab-Yum tankas) directly depict the sexual interpenetration of God and Goddess, but as a way of visually representing the sacred marriage of such fundamental aspects of Buddhist Dharma as skillful means and wisdom, or compassion and emptiness.

Could the emergence of a Divine Pair in our collective awareness provide images and ceremonies that would directly embrace the power of this ancient wisdom about sacred marriage? Could the emergence of a Divine Pair create a rebirth of sacred marriage widely accessible to those who choose relationship as a spiritual path?

We can speculate.

The appearance of a Divine Pair in the culture's collective Imaginal Realm is a natural evolution of our heritage of sacred marriage. The emergence of the Divine Pair will expand and make available this traditional wisdom to many couples on the transcending path in order to guide them on their challenging journey into Third Presence. The constellation of the Divine Pair archetype will inspire new sacred art and ceremony—including the celebrations that initiate sacred marriage.

An Impromptu Marriage Ceremony

Several years ago, a group of couples, all of whom had been doing transcending relationship practices for some time, decided to come together for a new round of exploration and mutual reflection. As the weekend unfolded, we saw that the natural culmination of the three days together would be a ceremony of sacred marriage. All the couples were already married, so we envisioned this ceremony as a commitment to further expand our awareness of Third Presence.

After meeting altogether in council, we decided to break up into men's and women's circles first to make preparations for the ceremony. We agreed then to come together and, without any further planning, move into spontaneous expressions of our deepening commitment. We trusted that our Thirds would guide us towards the celebration of union that was appropriate for the twelve of us at that moment in our lives.

Most of the time spent in the separate circles involved clarification of our intentions, emotional clearing, physical purification, and getting ourselves properly costumed for the big event. The men and women had no idea what the other group was cooking up. We arrived back in the "chapel" with more laughter than nervousness, anticipating that something delightful was about to happen.

The first portion of the ceremony involved admiring each other's attire (which might be described generously as "shamanic") and sharing in words and song what it meant for men and women to enter the path of sacred marriage. At no time did it occur to us to conduct six separate ceremonies or imitate the wedding rituals we had all gone through before. We talked of dedicating our relationships to sustaining all forms of life on the planet and recommitting ourselves to the practices. We talked about mutually supporting each other's relationships in the future as a Circle of Lovers. The strong connections we had just made at the men's and women's circles were maintained, even as we moved towards our celebration of union.

At the culmination of the ceremony, we spontaneously formed two lines, men on one side, women on the other, as if a traditional contra dance was about to begin. Each couple called on their Third to witness their vows and act as minister in blessing the union. We spoke of the "Circle of Thirds" and sensed that all of our otherworldly allies were now in cahoots with each other. When the first couple stepped forward to speak their vows, the rest of us spontaneously formed a circle around the initiates. The woman's vows were affirmed by her sisters with "Ho's" and short verbal elaborations. The men supported their brothers in a similar manner. Then we reformed the lines and the second couple stepped forward.

Although each set of vows was different, a common thread joined them all. We recognized this commonality, but at no time then or later did anyone feel that the uniqueness of their relationship was compromised. When everyone had spoken their vows, we asked that all the Thirds jointly give the empowering blessing for our unions in the name of the Divine Pair.

In this shared state of Third Presence, no one felt inhibited from sharing the images and words we heard from our "ministers" as they gave guidance and blessings. The shadow sides of our relationships were well represented in each Third's teachings. The ceremony ended much as an inspired Quaker Meeting, with affirmations and admonitions coming through all of us spontaneously. Toasts, breaking of wine glasses, dancing, and food followed. We felt recommitted, not only to our partners, but also to our newly created circle of co-pilgrims on the transcending path.

The Evolution of Marriage

The unique qualities of this experience, aspects of which have reappeared in other ceremonies in which we have participated, permit a few speculations about the evolution of sacred marriage and the rites of passage in a transcending relationship.

- Marriage for those on the transcending path will include entry into a global community of lovers.[9]

- The acknowledged true guides and ministers to the marriage will be unseen residents of the Imaginal Realm. As a result, the tone of the sacred marriage journey will be one of humility, rather than the joining of two egos to form yet a larger egoistic structure called "a couple."

- Women and men will see themselves less individualistically and more as archetypal man and woman. They will not break with their genders in creating the union (as some men and women now do) but heal the separation of genders through the practices of their marriage.

- Each partnership will see itself as a manifestation of the Divine Pair. Being married will mean joining a group of peers with a core vision that evolves through interaction among the couples.

- Couples will be less inclined to hide their darkest difficulties and more open about sharing their struggles. The tendency to live the shadow parts of their relation-

[9] Although largely forgotten, this vision of marriage is not new and remnants of it still appear in conventional ceremonies. In many nineteenth-century Eastern European Jewish communities, for example, the newly married partners went visiting immediately after the ceremony, introducing themselves to every family in the village and, in turn, being received as new members of the adult community

ships in isolation from each other (so prevalent now) will be replaced by an openness and sharing that will accelerate working through the many challenges along the transcending path.

• Establishing appropriate erotic boundaries among couples and singles will be motivated by the sense of gender identification ("brotherhood and sisterhood") and empowered by honest communication within the community. Supported by ongoing relationship practices, these forces of integrity will slowly replace the existing—and overtaxed—moral codes that are based primarily on limiting personal behavior.

• One of the consequences of the growing sense of community and openness among couples will be a more lighthearted attitude about relationship and marriage that will go a long way towards making the journey more pleasurable.

Epilogue
Walking at Dusk
• Our Third Tells a Story •

Our Third is an old soul
Slightly weary, but wiser
From its time with us

Well-chosen by the Mistress and Master
To guide our love
Towards the great crossing

We are being shown how to navigate
That river's currents and eddies
Through trust and timeless love

I am ready to make that voyage with you
My Mystery, my forever surprise of light and dark
My Buddy

I will love you on the river—and beyond

*S*ometimes Jack and Jaquelyn walk along the road built for the big trucks that used to rumble by hourly hauling sugar cane. Often they walk in silence, communicating through images with the row of ironwood trees that speak eloquently when the trades are blowing or with the unseen beings that appear at dusk. As the light fades, the land spirits invite those who walk to observe details in the landscape that they have failed to notice before. Sometimes they challenge walkers to pay attention to a truth about themselves or their relationships. If they speak fiercely enough, the walkers may feel a twinge of fear being alone and vulnerable in the spirits' domain. On those occasions the walkers quicken their pace and return to the safety of the house.

Now a week after Jack and Jaquelyn arrived, they are taking their first walk together. Both are delighted to be freed from the tensions of leaving and the stress of the previous few months.

• I am delighted, too. It has not been easy trying to make contact with them. •

The air is balmy and a hint of orange already colors the banks of clouds that inevitably pile up against the slopes of the massive mountain to the west. The couple walk past familiar guavas, ohia, and rose apple woven generously with passion fruit vines. In a moment of joyous appreciation of being there and alone together, they stop, make eye contact, and silently count their blessings.

The couple's exuberance stirs the land spirits. The guava and rose apple remember them; the ironwoods offer a greeting. They stop and listen to the familiar call of the mourning doves and the chatter of the smaller birds. The silence is full of messages. The man hears the slight ringing in his ears that signals a transition in consciousness.

"I need your help with something," he says. The woman looks up expectantly. He doesn't begin many conversations that way, she thinks. "I'm still dealing with turning sixty-five and worrying about what's going on in my body. Even though all the tests have come back negative so far, mortality is still on my mind. We've talked about it many times, but the bottom line is that I'm still carrying some fear about death."

"I'm much more afraid about a long painful dying than death itself," the woman offers.

"I know. That's why I'm asking for support. I've always had the feeling that you were more comfortable with death than I, probably in part because you're a woman."

• I draw closer. It has been a long time since I really had their attention. In a few moments both of them realize that they are no longer alone, no longer in just a dialogue. As they feel my presence, our joint awareness expands. •

"Probably," the woman answers, sensing a movement out of the corner of her eye in the old clumps of cane along the road. "Childbirth connects us to the beginning of life and I suppose to the end as well. If we carry the mystery of birth in our wombs, the mystery of death must be close too...There are creatures all around us, you know."

• After a moment of silence, I send the man a message, which is received as a picture. •

"I just had a vivid image of you holding me as I'm dying. I feel completely at peace. There's no fear. The uneasiness I've been feeling is gone. I've had many images of you holding me before, but not as a way of dispelling my apprehension about death."

"I think I'll be making the crossing before you," the woman says.

• Don't take the image too literally, I say inside their heads. •

"It doesn't matter who goes first," the man says. "The strongest feeling in the image is how much we love each other. I've been hearing this ever since I can remember—in books, poetry, scripture. Surrendering completely to loving the other vanquishes the fear of death."

"That's one of Jesus' major teachings," the woman says. The man nods.

• I open the door further. •

"Then our challenge is to enter that world of love before we die," the man says with some intensity. "I hope we have enough years left to learn how to make the crossing without any fear."

"If we reach that place, we'll be able to continue our relationship after we die," the woman says matter-of-factly. "I'm not sure in what way exactly."

• I nod, which they feel but, of course, do not see. •

"That's probably why we've been doing so much shadow work these past few months. There seems to be less tolerance now for our old patterns. They're getting tedious."

• You can say that again, I transmit. •

"It does get boring," the woman agrees. "We have to discover some kind of 'Elderhood Yoga' to prepare us for the crossing."

"Yes, Elderhood Yoga, or maybe we should call it *Crossing Yoga*," the man responds. "We have to find new practices that will help us make a smooth crossing, without fear and with enough consciousness to be able to continue our relationship on the other side—assuming that's possible."

"I'm sure it is," the woman says, again, matter-of-factly. "I love the term Crossing Yoga. After all, one doesn't have to be an elder to approach death consciously. I've noticed lately that our lovemaking is changing. There's more happening between our subtle bodies and less on the physical. Your erection isn't quite as hard as it used to be. Of course, it could be just declining testosterone."

"I thought my testosterone test came out normal."

"I was just kidding. Sometimes you don't get my humor."

• I send them a "don't get into it" message. •

"It's perfect that our lovemaking is moving in that direction," the woman continues. "We're learning to make love more fully in the Imaginal Realm, so we can eventually detach from the physical."

"In preparation for making love after we cross."

"You have a one track mind—only kidding, only kidding. It's almost dark. Let's continue this in council when we get back and invite the Third. Maybe we can listen more attentively now that we've begun to unwind."

• I thought you'd never ask, I transmit. •

The light is fading, as they walk on in silence for a while and then climb up the long dirt driveway. The mourning doves celebrate the end of day. Only a touch of pink remains in the west. The air has turned a bit chilly. A three-quarter moon breaks through the clouds and lights their way.

"Don't put on the lights. The council candle will be enough," the woman says as they enter the house.

The council is dedicated to the spirits of the land and learning about Crossing Yoga. The man and the woman sit quietly for a few moments and then put the talking piece in front of the third pillow. "Let's hear what our friend has to say about all this," the man says.

• Their invitation connects me with source and permits the transmission of teachings from the Divine Pair...

• You are on the right track when you speak of the Yoga of Crossing. It is time for both of you to begin the journey towards freedom and nonattachment to physical form. To begin with, you must continue letting go of your identification with lifelong roles and patterns. These have helped to hold your lives and relationship together, but now, as you approach the crossing, Eros no longer needs such structures. A new cohesion is arising that you already know in your lovemaking and in councils such as this. But you will come to know it in a more continuous and empowered way in the future, if you are attentive to the new practices that will be shown to you.

• More explicitly, it is the erotic cohesion between your subtle bodies that will slowly take the place of the old ways of connecting. This erotic magnetism will maintain much of the coherence in the future and is essential to the proper transformation of the relationship at the crossing and beyond. Put another way, the challenge is to learn to live more comfortably in the Imaginal Realm, while continuing to perform your service to yourselves and others who live in the physical world.

• There are several important implications of this increasing focus on your subtle bodies. First, the relationship is to be conducted more on the level of energy interaction and less on the level of verbal and emotional processing. You already have received this message, but your attachment to verbal interaction has been strong—and properly so. Many people have benefited from the council practices you have shared and more will continue to do so in the future. But the two of you need to begin shifting your perspective. More silent time in council is needed in order to listen to me and others whose image manifestations reside in the Imaginal Realm. Put still greater emphasis on the energetic level in your ordinary interactions and in carrying out your practices, as you have been doing for some time during lovemaking. Learn the art of "being in the field of your relationship" when you are physically apart. That capability is an important part of Crossing Yoga.

• Secondly, you both need to develop individual practices that will facilitate detachment from physical reality. Your emphasis in the past has been appropriately on the interactive nature of relationship, and you have become reasonably skilled at that. Now it is time to develop additional practices that will bring each of you more peace, inspiration, and creative energy in fulfilling your service. Reflecting imperfections you see in each other has been a strong practice for you both. Now it is time to balance this skill with the ability to let the Divine Pair directly manifest in your life together and in your work with others. Use what you have called "deity yoga" to expand your visionary capabilities. This may seem difficult at first, but the practices for accomplishing this will become available, I assure you.

• My relationship with you will change accordingly. In the past you have seen me as teacher, comforter, challenger, and shaman. We have communicated mostly on the etheric level of your subtle bodies. Now we must begin to explore more refined portions of the Imaginal Realm that involve your visionary imaginations and other higher mental faculties. Gradually, we will work less on the etheric level, which is still quite connected to the physical world. In short, I will be less teacher and shaman, and more emissary of the Divine Pair. This is the natural evolution of my work with you and will lead to a more radical change as you approach the crossing—but I cannot talk about that any further at this time.

• Third and finally, your work with others will be based more on *transmission* and less on the more familiar process that you call transference. Although performing service for others will continue to be the core of your life right up to the crossing—and beyond, I might add—this will not be accomplished with the same intense effort, that it is now. The degree of activity you both indulge in at present is unbecoming to elders exploring the Yoga of Crossing. There are times when your hyperactivity and compulsiveness is quite unappealing to me. In two words, *lighten up*. What you have to bring to others will be conveyed by a process of clear energetic transmission that you will find more artful and effective than the effort, however devoted, so familiar to you now.

• I do not mean to be harsh. Generally you have been more than attentive to your work both individually and with each other. But it is time to make a transition into another mode of service. Nurture and be more attentive to your subtle bodies when you interact with others and also when you are alone. The strong intentions you have set for the remainder of your lives cannot be achieved by working primarily in the physical domain. They require you to become more skilled working in the Imaginal Realm. I and others will do our part, but you must carry out the practices that will be revealed to you over the next year or two.

• That is enough for now. I have greatly appreciated this opportunity to serve your relationship. It is not often I have such spaciousness in which to enter your busy lives. You can best serve your intentions now by celebrating the Divine Pair through what you call sexual communion. You will have new words for all this as time goes on, although your present terminology is more than adequate.

• It has not always been easy being part of this triad—your relationship is a great challenge. But I have relished every minute of our journey together. I learn, too, you know. As emissary, I, too, am a student of the Divine Pair. Now play and enjoy your bodies fully—both physical and subtle—while you still inhabit them. •

The man and the woman talk about what they had heard in the council. They are surrounded by moonlight entering through the large windows. After a while, they put out the candle and prepare once again to encounter the Mystery.

Appendix 1
The Soul, the Imaginal Realm, and Visionary Imagination

*I*t is difficult to find language for describing events or phenomena that are not visible to ordinary perception. So it is in portraying the life of the soul. Certainly we experience consciousness extending beyond ordinary reality through dreams, meditation, and other psychic events. Although it is natural for poets and metaphysicians to talk about these experiences as if they had entered a different world, we need to remind ourselves regularly that these "realms" in fact refer to non-ordinary states of awareness.

In mystical psychology the soul is defined as the imperishable part of us that precedes and survives body, emotions, and mind. Death is often seen as a release of the soul from its imprisonment in this worldly attire. The soul is that part of us that touches and feels touched by the divine, whatever name it is given. Love, beauty, profound sorrow, deep feelings of reverence, joy in nature, and great art are routes to contacting the soul. Sri Aurobindo said that the soul is the eternal essence or spark that dwells at the center of our being in the secret heart between the mind and the emotions.[1] Alice Bailey, through her channeling of the discarnate "Tibetan" Djwhal Khul, speaks of the soul as that which calls back the body at death.[2]

The transcendent nature of soul and its connection with love is deeply embedded in the roots of Western culture. In *Symposium*, Plato referred to love or Eros as a spiritual intermediary between that which is mortal and that which is immortal. He believed it is uniquely by means of love that dialogue takes place between the human soul and the gods. He repeatedly emphasized that the most important human activity is to "tend the soul." In brief: *Our soul is the intermediary between our humanity and God.* The realm of the soul, although intangible, exists as a real intermediate state of consciousness between ordinary awareness and full awareness of spirit.

Radical Sufism

The radical Sufis, who lived during the beginning of the second millennium, believed that the Godhead itself possesses the ultimate power of creative imagination. They felt that by imagining the universe, God actually created it. The Sufis taught that the imagination is essential for dialogue with the divine. The imagination was said to be the instrument of the soul, just as the hand, for example, is an instrument of the physical body.

The French Islamic scholar and mystic Henry Corbin translated and interpreted several of these twelfth- and thirteenth-century Islamic esotericists, particularly the prolific Ibn 'Arabi. In his translations, it was Corbin who first called the Sufi vision of the human soul's habitat the *Imaginal World*.[3] According to Ibn

---

[1] See *The Psychic Being: Soul, Its Nature, Mission and Evolution*, Sri Aurobindo and The Mother, Lotus Light Publications, 1990; and *Savitri: A Legend and a Symbol*, Sri Aurobindo and The Mother, Sri Aurobindo Trust, 1970 (first published in 1951).
[2] *Death: The Great Adventure*, Alice A. Bailey, Lucus Publishing, 1985.
[3] See *Creative Imagination in the Sufism of Ibn 'Arabi*, Henry Corbin, Princeton University Press, 1989; and *Spiritual Body and Celestial Earth*, Henry Corbin, Princeton University Press, 1977.

'Arabi and other Sufis, the Imaginal Realm is just one of several hierarchical planes of being they called the *Presences*. The First Presence is the world of the Absolute Mystery; the Second Presence is the angelic world of the spirits or the Holy Spirit; the Third Presence is the world of celestial souls, archetypes, and ultimate principles (e.g. yin/yang). The Fourth Presence is the imaginal world of idea-images (personifications of archetypes), the luminous *alam al-mithal* (literally, "middle world"). The higher or finer realms of this Fourth Presence include the paradises and heavens; the lower, the hells of the many religions. All of it together is called the soul-world or Imaginal Realm. The Fifth Presence is our physical world, which includes ordinary material reality together with the denser aspects of what we have been calling the etheric domain.

Occultists vary in their terminology. Some equate the Imaginal Realm with the *astral plane*, while others identify only the lower realms containing the hells with the astral. According to Ibn 'Arabi the Imaginal is the realm of human souls containing archetypal forms but made up of immaterial or "subtle" matter. This fourth world of idea-images he called the world beyond the ordinary senses, a world in which spirits are materialized (descending from the spirit realm of the first three Presences) and bodies spiritualized (ascending from the physical world). These ascents and descents—that is, transformations between physical and nonmaterial forms—take place through our active imagination (or what we have been calling visionary imagination), which is seen as the perceptual organ and dominant creative force in the Fourth Presence. Ibn 'Arabi considered the Imaginal Realm to be the principal intermediary plane, accessible to humans, between the Absolute Mystery and our visible physical world.

This prolific mystic also proposed that, in the descent from Absolute Mystery to the physical domain, the harvest of each Presence is the one immediately following it in the descending hierarchy. More precisely, each level of reality is created as a projected image or reflection of the one preceding it and, therefore, is already present in its predecessor in a different form. We might say simply that the levels of reality are "nested." Thus our physical reality, for example, already exists, moment to moment, in the Imaginal Realm.

It is interesting to compare this vision with what Ken Wilber proposes about human evolution. In *The Atman Project*,[4] he says that at each moment in our evolution, the entirety of the then existing state of collective consciousness is a part of the consciousness at the next stage of growth. Wilber concludes that *development* and *transcendence* are two different words for describing the process of moving from unconsciousness, through self-awareness, towards superconsciousness and ultimate unity with spirit. He feels that every human's capacity for expanded consciousness and the accompanying ubiquitous desire for this unity are balanced by a fear of the loss of identity (or even life itself) at the previous stage of development. He suggests that this is precisely what draws so many of us to the visionary path, with its reassuring use of symbolic forms (images) and sounds (mantra) rather than the starker less sensual ascetic routes to wholeness.

We can now begin to understand why this traditional visionary perspective is so important for the evolution of intimate relationship. The stage of relational consciousness we have called secular is centered in the physical domain of reality. Because of the nested nature of the hierarchy of awareness, the next, more expanded, stage of relationship includes the entire array of secular functioning—plus much more. The initiation of this level can be achieved through use of the basic practices of the visionary path that are natural to mature relationship (unlike ascetic practices). As we have described, visionary practices in relationship include joint meditation and energy exchange, the sharing of dreams, dyadic council, and the combination of awakened eroticism and heightened use of imaginative faculties. Such practices can inspire two loving partners to enter the Imaginal Realm and create a unifica-

---

[4] *The Atman Project: A Transpersonal View of Human Development*, Ken Wilber, Theosophical Publishing House, 1980.

tion of their visionary, meditative, and erotic lives. This is why we have spoken of evolving beyond secular relationship as the *transcending path*.

There are further subtleties in the analogy between the transcending path of relationship and the love affair of the radical Sufis with the divine. In Islamic Sufism the heart is seen as the locus of spiritual perception or what we have been calling visionary imagination. Ibn 'Arabi taught that in spiritual perception we see/create real figures with the imagination that actually exist in the Imaginal Realm. In fact, he believed that the kind of knowledge this intermediary world has to offer is most naturally gained through visionary perception or what is sometimes called inner revelation.

The ultimate practice of creative imagination was thought to be dialogical prayer, in contrast to the unidirectional forms of prayer, worship, and idolatry. For the radical Sufis, prayerful meditation was the main entryway into creative imagination and the Imaginal Realm. Corbin coined the term *imaginal* in order to distinguish visionary imagination from fantasy or fictional imagination, and he went to great lengths to differentiate imaginative consciousness from figments of the mind, which he called unreal or utopian.

Carl Jung makes the same distinction. In his writings on analytical psychology he says that imagination is an image-making, form-giving creative activity in contrast to fantasy, which he calls fleeting and entirely personal. In Jung's words[5]: "A fantasy is more or less your own invention, and remains on the surface of personal things and conscious expectations. But active imagination, as the term denotes, means that the images have a life of their own and that symbolic events develop according to their own logic."

---

[5] *Analytical Psychology: Its Theory and Practice*, C.G. Jung, Vintage Books, 1968.

To paraphrase Corbin: spiritual knowledge of the Imaginal Realm is obtained in the form of images that exist, even though invisible, as "flesh of the spirit."

James Hillman honors Corbin's interpretations of radical Sufism and reiterates that visionary imagination has *theophanic power*—that is, the ability to make the divine face visible. He agrees with Corbin that the heart *sees* spirit through a process of imagination: "Love is of the spirit, quickening the soul to its images in the heart."[6]

Similarly, in a transcending relationship the wisdom along this joint path of the heart is perceived primarily through an imaginative process that is heightened or fueled by an awakened eroticism. This marriage of eroticism and imaginative capacity creates a tangible connection to the Imaginal Realm. Thus, *heightened sexuality in a transcending relationship is the lovers' dialogical prayer and a primary way for them to enter the Imaginal Realm.* We believe that the spiritual perceptions in a transcending relationship (for example, encounters with the Third) are neither illusory nor figments of the mind. Rather they represent direct observations, by means of visionary imagination, of the connection between the mystery of a particular relationship and the Mystery of the Divine.

Western Views of the Imaginal Realm

We need not rely solely on Eastern spiritual traditions to inspire or support practices for embracing the Imaginal Realm. One of the most influential Western explorers of non-ordinary realities and multidimensional consciousness, American psychologist William James, stated in his seminal work, *Varieties of Religious Experience*[7]:

---

[6] *The Thought of the Heart*, James Hillman, Eranos Lectures 2, Spring Publications, 1981, p. 18.
[7] *The Varieties of Religious Experiences*, William James, Random House, Modern Library Edition, 1936, p. 506 (first published in 1902).

The further limits of our being plunge, it seems to me, into an altogether other dimension of existence from the sensible and merely "understandable" world. Name it the mystical region, or the supernatural region, whichever you choose...the unseen region in question is not merely ideal, for it produces effects in this world. When we commune with it, work is actually done upon our finite personality, for we are turned into new men, and consequences in the way of conduct follow in the natural world upon regenerative change. But that which produces effects within another reality must be termed a reality itself, so I feel as if we have no philosophical excuse for calling the unseen of mystical world unreal.

Rudolf Steiner also dealt with the difficulty of living in the ordinary reality of contemporary civilization while aspiring to the knowledge of what he called the higher worlds (the equivalent of Ibn 'Arabi's first four Presences).[8] Steiner taught that by means of meditation we can activate and become aware of that eternal quality in each of us that is altered neither by birth nor death. He called this the soul and felt that artistic introspection combined with meditation was the path to uncovering this secret core beneath superficial layers of physical reality. In the world of the soul, feelings and thoughts react to each other, he said, just as physical entities do in ordinary reality.

At the same time, Steiner emphasized that the investigation of higher worlds should not dilute our participation in the demands of everyday life. On the contrary, he felt we should conduct our spiritual search in the context of worldly consciousness to avoid the confusion and instability that can occur when unexpected external forces interrupt a person overly focused on the Imaginal Realm. For Steiner (as for so many others), the key to maintaining harmony with natural physical laws and tangible reality is the

[8] *Knowledge of Higher Worlds and Its Attainment*, Rudolf Steiner, Anthroposophic Press, 1947.

activation and development of the heart center. He believed that, only then, can we transform the earth by seeding it with what we learn spiritually.

Towards this end, Steiner taught that the chakras are the "sense-organs" of the soul. In particular, he said that a well-developed sexual chakra provides the necessary equilibrium between body, soul, and spirit. This supports our own experience that a strong erotic capacity is the foundation of a transcending relationship.

Emanuel Swedenborg, another prolific explorer of the Imaginal Realm, believed spiritual capacity to be the basis of psychological reality. His research into multidimensional consciousness and the Imaginal Realm was conducted while in a trance state, which he induced through meditation and subtle deep breathing practices. As a result of his personal explorations, Swedenborg concluded that human lives involve constant interaction with a hierarchy of spirits that are related to feelings about ourselves and others.

Swedenborg concluded that creation is a continuous series of God's images. Our visible universe is nothing more than a theatrical representation of the Lord's kingdom. He believed that the world of spirit constantly interacts with our mind processes, which take place on various levels corresponding to those of the spiritual world. These levels or dimensions of consciousness include pure feelings (not to be confused with emotions), thoughts and ideas, speech and gestures, and bodily functioning.

Unlike many other explorers of the Imaginal Realm, Swedenborg dealt with the spiritual nature of intimate relationship in a profound way. His trance meditations led him to conclude that human love is the ultimate proof of God's omnipresence.[9] He found that the movement of heaven is towards oneness, achieved through joining with and loving others, while the gen-

---

[9] *Conjugal Love: The Delights of Wisdom*, Emanuel Swedenborg, Swedenborg Press, 1949 (written in 1768).

eral drift of hell is toward separation, division, isolation, and non-relationship.

In sex and love Swedenborg perceived a principle that operates beyond the human condition throughout all creation. He viewed truly conjugal love as a union of souls and a conjunction of minds. In the heavenly realms two married partners are called *two* when mentioned as husband and wife, and *one* when spoken of as angels. He believed this was the meaning of "They are no more twain, but one flesh."[10]

In more recent years, the surge of interest in so-called paranormal phenomena has created an entirely different context for embracing the existence of non-ordinary reality. Out-of-body experiences (also called astral travel), lucid or conscious dreaming, ESP (clairvoyance and clairaudience), psychokinesis, and physical materialization all lend credence to the existence of subtle levels of human consciousness. These psychic capabilities are often associated with the opening of a strong connection between the sexual chakra and the brow center.

As a result of his extensive investigation of near-death experience, Kenneth Ring concludes that these events, as well as UFO encounters, take place in what he calls *alternate realities*. He emphasizes that this is not a spatial reality but an imaginal realm. In a July 1992 interview, Ring stated[11]:

> The distinction that is made about imaginal realities is they have a matrix or structure to them, and you can tune in to them if you have the right faculty of perception. If you are already sensitized to these imaginal realms, then your imagination, acting like an organ of perception in its own right, can simply detect these realities.

Ring feels that both near-death experiences and authentic UFO encounters exemplify *initiatory journeys* that are part of an

---

[10] Matthew, xix 6.
[11] "The Cosmic Connection," a *New Age Journal* interview with Kenneth Ring, conducted by Jonathan Adolf and Peggy Taylor, July/August, 1992.

evolution of humanity toward higher consciousness.[12] Knowing we're ignoring the welfare of the planet, our deep unconscious is sending us a collective wake-up call through these kinds of occurrences, Ring believes.

Dangers in Exploring the Imaginal Realm

As many mystics have taught, the journey into the Imaginal Realm can be dangerous. According to Ken Wilber[13]: "Between the Existential Level [physical reality] and the Level of Mind [Ibn `Arabi's Third Presence] lies the most mysterious, unexplored, misunderstood, fear-inducing, and generally puzzling portion of the spectrum—the Transpersonal Bands." Wilber says these intermediate realms of consciousness (which are included in what we have been calling the Imaginal Realm) can be experienced either as the *dark night of the soul* or *boundless light*. Here one can meet bodhisattvas and angels or be accosted by evil forces. Wilber believes one usually enters the Transpersonal Bands carrying the maps previously created on the biosocial and ego levels of personal consciousness. To a large extent, these maps determine how the territory is viewed.

Many spiritual teachers have warned novitiates to stay away from the seduction of imagery and paranormal spiritual phenomena. Some gurus imply that a spiritual aspirant can survive the transition through these realms only by surrendering to a teacher (such as the guru) who has already completed the journey and, as a consequence, can help the disciple face its dangers.

Yet Aurobindo said, "None can reach heaven who has not passed through hell."[14] He believed that if these mid-regions of consciousness are to be feared because of intrinsic danger or wrong

---

[12] *The Omega Project: Near-Death Experiences, UFO Encounters, and Mind at Large*, Kenneth Ring, William Morrow & Co, 1992.
[13] *The Spectrum of Consciousness*, Ken Wilber, Theosophical Publishing House, 1977, p. 266.
[14] *Savitri*, Sri Aurobindo, Sri Aurobindo Ashram Trust, 1970, p. 227.

use, all of spirituality should also be placed on the same alert. In any event, he emphasizes that right attitude, discrimination, training, and discipline are required. He felt that these were indispensable for those endeavoring to create the "life divine" here on earth.

Our view is that the dangers of the non-physical realms involve disowned shadow elements in the personal or, for some practitioners, the collective unconscious. The great power with which material from the Imaginal Realm can suddenly enter our physical reality (for example, a vivid image directing us to take action, perhaps even violent action), make it essential that each of us deals with our personal shadow issues as an organic part of the exploration of expanded consciousness—no matter what our spiritual path.

Obviously an intense and productive way of exploring the personal shadow is through a mature erotic relationship. Doing the hard work of relating generates enormous amounts of energy that, when channeled through the practices we have described, provides the necessary empowerment for a couple's journey along the path of transcending relationship.

Appendix 2
A Brief History of
Non-orgasmic Sexuality

*T*here is strong historical precedence for the practice of sexual intercourse in which the man withholds seminal ejaculation. Non- discharging sexuality has been practiced for centuries as a form of meditation in the tantrism of Hinduism and Tibetan Buddhism. In Hindu tantrism the female is seen as a vehicle for the male priest's sexual meditation. However, little has been written about the practice from the woman's perspective, although in the beginning, her role was probably as a highly trained temple priestess. In most of the Buddhist tantric literature, the sexual embrace—*maithuna* or Yab-Yum—is seen primarily as the union of male and female principles. Again, there is relatively little focus on the ceremony from the woman's point of view.

When the cultures surrounding these practices grew more patriarchal, the resulting devaluation of women and separation between sexuality and spirituality put an end to the tradition of the sexual priestess.[1] Women could only be seen as sacred if they were virgins or married. The practice of maithuna, for example,

---

[1] This tradition is sometimes referred to as the divine or sacred prostitute; see *The Sacred Prostitute*, Nancy Qualls-Corbett, Inner City Books, 1988.

was restricted primarily to married couples and is still practiced to a limited extent in the East.

The separation between sexuality and spirituality continues to be emphasized in contemporary Buddhist teachings. For example, Lama Govinda stresses that the female Bodhisattvas in the Buddhist mandalas represent wisdom, knowledge, and the spiritual attitude of unification, but have nothing to do with physical sexuality.[2] He rejects the basic idea of Shaktism[3] and its "world-creating eroticism" and goes on to say, "Instead of seeking union with a woman outside ourselves, we have to seek it within ourselves by the union of our male and female nature in the process of meditation."

In Chinese and Taoist sexual literature, now more familiar in the West, various non-ejaculatory yogas are offered as practices that engender harmony, longevity, and immortality. The Taoists, in particular, see the body as a sacred laboratory of the spirit, although not necessarily in the context of relationship. In some schools the *pair* ceremonies were seen as a transition to the *purer* practice of harmonizing yin and yang in the body of an individual practitioner.

Much of the early Taoist literature teaches that the positive vital energy that floods the body and the surrounding field during sexual intercourse is lost when the male ejaculates. The retaining of the semen was believed to renew spiritual life in the man, just as the ejaculate, when released into the woman, participates in the creation of new physical life. In some early teachings, the woman was encouraged to have as many orgasms as possible, which the man utilized to enhance his energy during the ceremony. Male sexual prowess was seen as the ability to stimulate and expand the sexual energy with one's partner while simultaneously conserving

---

[2] See *Foundations of Tibetan Mysticism*, Lama Anagarika Govinda, Samuel Weiser, 1960, p. 99-103.
[3] The worship of Shakti, who in the tantric tradition is the universal female power endowed with all aspects of life. When Shakti, representing kinetic energy, unites with Shiva, her eternal partner, their sexual interpenetration "gives rise to all of creation." See *The Tantric Way*, Ajit Mookerjee and Madhu Khanna, Thames and Hudson, 1977.

semen. Although the man's process in these classical teachings was given more attention than the woman's, sexual compatibility was still seen as the foundation of conjugal harmony. While the non-ejaculatory traditions flourished, women were often highly valued as sexual teachers who initiated men (particularly royalty) into the practice.

In his excellent anthology of classical Chinese sexology,[4] Douglas Wile says of Mantak Chia's writings[5]: "Like many observers of the West, Chia finds that sexuality is the chief obsession of our culture, but comes to the original conclusion that, because of this, perhaps only sex itself can serve as a vehicle for the spiritual awakening of the masses." Wile also quotes from Stephen Chang's writings[6]: "By following the Tao of Sexology, mankind will eventually incarnate God's nature to its fullest."

In another less well-known treatise on sexuality, J. William Lloyd describes non-seminal or "controlled" intercourse as a way of "soul- blending."[7] He attributes the discovery and application of this art to John Humphrey Noyes, the founder of the Oneida Community.[8] Lloyd pleads with his readers in a poetic way to consider the controlled practice of making love and advocates that both the man and woman withhold orgasm while remaining in deep interpenetration. He says, "If you do not come nearer heaven in this act and relation than in anything else you do or ever will do, you fail of perfect Karezza."

Some years ago, the contemporary Western spiritual teacher Da Free John was a strong and articulate advocate for what he

---

[4] *The Art of the Bedchamber: The Chinese Sexual Yoga Classics Including Women's Solo Meditation Texts*, State University of New York Press, 1992.
[5] *Taoist Secrets of Love: Cultivating Male Sexual Energy*, Mantak Chia, Aurora Press, 1984.
[6] *The Tao of Sexology: The Book of Infinite Wisdom*, Stephen Chang, Tao Publishing, 1986.
[7] *The Karezza Method, or Magnetation: The Art of Connubial Love*, J. William Lloyd, self-published, 1931.
[8] Lloyd started the community in Putney, Vermont in 1842, but because of its controversial practice of "complex marriage," was forced to move to Oneida, New York, five years later. The Oneida community was made up of farmers and mechanics who collectively developed an agricultural and blacksmith business that prospered until 1980, when pressure from neighbors resulted in Lloyd moving to Canada.

called regenerative sexuality or sexual communion. (Subsequently, he advocated sexual abstinence, especially for his more advanced disciples.) In *Love of the Two-Armed Form*, John emphasizes that the conventional practice of orgasm is degenerative except for purposes of conception.[9] He goes on to say that when ejaculation is withheld, the transformed orgasm serves to awaken the higher functions of the brain. Then there is no longer any need to choose between God and sex, since one's sexual relationship can be carried out as a form of God-communion: "The right use of the intensification generated through sexual play is to consciously inhale, receive, relax, exhale, release and so control the energy of the approaching crisis, allowing it to move from the concentrated area of the genitals and to permeate or pervade the whole body, one's lover, and the whole world to infinity."[10]

John proposed that sexual communion is a transitional evolutionary process that guides us into the psychic and actively spiritual stage of life and then drops away completely as the practitioner remains in constant "Love-Communion with the Living God" (the name, by the way, that he came to give himself).

In a transcending relationship, the practice of sexual communion not only connects each partner with spirit but also with the divine presence in the other. Lovemaking without discharge empowers visionary imagination in a new way, interweaves the subtle and physical bodies, and harmonizes minds and emotions. We believe that *the practice of sexual communion is constantly evolving and, therefore, is its own transition to greater God-communion.* For those who choose the path of transcending relationship (rather than the traditional path of the individual disciple, for example), we believe it will not be necessary—or even natural—to let go of their sexual practice in order to develop further spiritually.

---

[9] *Love of the Two-Armed Form: The Free and Regenerative Function of Sexuality in True Religious or Spiritual Practice*, Bubba Free John, Dawn Horse Press, 1978.
[10] *Ibid.*, p. 234-235.

Appendix 3
Shamanism and Relationship

*S*hamanism is probably as old as visionary consciousness and lies at the roots of all traditions that bridge the physical and spirit worlds. As described by Roger Walsh, the key features of shamanism are the voluntary entrance into altered states of consciousness, the ability to journey to other realms in these states, and acquiring knowledge or power there in order to help others.[1] Anthropologist Michael Harner states that the central focus of shamanism is "contact with an ordinarily hidden reality."[2]

By entering a state of trance, the traditional shaman journeys into the spirit domain for the purpose of healing physical or mental illness, understanding dreams, or receiving guidance for the community. Customarily, the trance is induced during sacred rituals by music (for example, drumming), dancing, chanting, breathing practices, and/or the use of ceremonial or sacred plants (such as peyote or ayahuasca). Characteristically, the shaman makes use of spirit allies, often in the form of power animals (wolf, raven, snake, for example) to gain the knowledge and strength needed to perform the healing as well as to protect the shaman during the journey. While in trance, the shaman is often substan-

---

[1] *The Spirit of Shamanism*, Roger N. Walsh, J.P. Tarcher, 1990.
[2] *The Way of the Shaman*, Michael Harner, Harper & Row, 1980.

tially out of body and, therefore, vulnerable to the dangers of the journey. These include being overwhelmed by dark forces in conflict with the intention to heal, losing the focus of intention during the journey, or being unable to understand the guidance received from the spirit domain.

The shaman is trained to see spirit in all forms of animate and inanimate life and, while in trance, can directly perceive and participate in the spirit realm. During the healing of an individual, for example, the shaman's emotions, feelings, and thoughts are expressed in a transpersonal way through the images of this visionary world. The shaman's task is to have sufficient awareness and control to interact with his or her own images as well as those arising from the body-mind of the person being healed. In some ways, the shamanic journey is analogous to entering into a conscious or lucid dream state. We might say that a shaman consciously enters another person's or the tribal dream world for the purpose of healing.

Shamanic healing is based on the interconnectedness of all forms of life and the accessibility to human consciousness of various levels of non-material as well as material reality. Shamanic practice involves the capacity to be aware of several of these levels of consciousness simultaneously.

The shamanic tradition is profoundly interwoven with the notion of the "wounded healer."[3] The wound might be connected with a spontaneous life experience, such as a life-threatening illness or accidental brush with death. In some traditions the wound is inflicted consciously as part of the shaman's initiation. In a real sense the wound is the shaman's doorway to the spirit world. Confronting this aspect of the dark side is an essential part of the shaman's ability to handle whatever arises on the spirit journey. With proper training, the wound teaches courage, humility, and appreciation for the mystical power of self-healing, all of which

---

[3] *Shaman: The Wounded Healer*, Joan Halifax, Thames & Hudson, 1982.

help to awaken the shaman's deepest creative and visionary capabilities.

On the personal level the shaman must overcome fear, doubt, and self-importance to practice healing or receive guidance from the spirit world. If there is unacknowledged doubt involved in the process, for example, the trance will be incomplete and the journey either aborted or terminated in failure. Traditionally the shaman travels alone, although often shamanic trance is induced during ceremonies involving other members of the community. The shaman usually lives at the "edge of the village," both figuratively and literally.

Despite the recent rebirth of interest, most Westerners are uncomfortable with shamanism's dramatic images and intimate contact with the world of animated spirits. Traditionally, the bridge between spirit and body in shamanic practices is expressed simply, dramatically, and without intellectual complexity. Despite our tendency to see shamanism as a primitive practice, the roots of our Western Judeo-Christian tradition are unmistakably shamanic, with ecstatic prayer and revelation taking the place of the shamanic trance and journey, respectively. Whatever else it is, the crucifixion of Jesus is also a version of the wounded healer story. One of Jesus' primary teachings—the Kingdom of Heaven is within—is a version of the shamanic teaching that everything in the universe is filled with the "spirit that dwells in all things."

We have found it inspiring and useful *to look at the transcending path of relationship as a shamanic journey in which the role of the shaman is played by the partners' Third.* Our dreams and work with many couples strongly suggest that the relationship between the physical and spiritual realms, created by the sacred marriage of Eros and Spirit, is fundamentally a shamanic partnership.

The state of loving union touched during deep sexuality, for example, can induce a trance state that is remarkably analogous to that of the shaman—with one possible exception. Although the state of ecstatic sexual union supports the healing of conflicts and disturbances of the mind-body and brings empowerment and guidance, it is *not* "out of body." On the other hand, since the eroticism in a transcending relationship is primarily focused on celebrating the relationship itself, rather than individual physical gratification, we might say that the trance of deep sexual communion is "out of the partners' ego-centered bodies."

The profound truth in the story of the wounded healer is also part of the reality of shamanic partnership. The transcending path requires that the partners be willing to confront the dark side of their individual personalities and their relationship with perseverance, courage, and respect for the risks involved. Healing the wounds created by the relationship itself (deep conflict, hurt, and betrayal, for example) can become the couple's path of initiation into greater contact with spirit as well as leading them to develop the ability to provide service to others.

As in the traditional shamanic path, fear, self-involvement, and doubt are the enemies of the shamanic partnership. Falling into a pattern of doubt about the relationship compromises the partners' abilities to transform it. The ally here is the profound trust that the challenges, however great they may be, are ultimately indigenous to the growth of the relationship and its ability to move along the transcending path. In the relational context, self-involvement can take the form of either partner being overly preoccupied with meeting individual needs or both becoming obsessed with the relationship itself. In the latter case, the partnership implodes and the transcendent quality (particularly in regard to the relationship's service to others) is soon lost.

The shamanic tradition leads naturally to a vision of reality that might be called the *Large Body*—a single complex organism that encompasses every manifestation of life (including each human being) as a part of its cellular structure. The Large Body provides a model of deity that gives the mind a visual image of the principle of interdependence and can help us feel part of something larger than our familiar "local reality."

The metaphor of the Large Body also provides a much needed reminder that the physical body plays a central role in our spiritual life and helps us avoid abstractions about spirituality and the deity that lead to the polarization of body and spirit. When we integrate the image of the Large Body, our concern for others is no longer just a moral imperative but arises out of the *physiological reality* of sharing a common organism. The Golden Rule is no longer a preacher's sermon but a common-sense truth. The Large Body's spirit and intelligence pervade each of its "cells," providing every one of us with the capacity for survival and regeneration through awareness of being a part of the all-embracing totality.

Appendix 4
Ancestors of the Divine Pair

Reviewing our cultural roots in Greek mythology, we were again reminded of the humanlike nature of the familiar Greek and Roman gods. We had forgotten the extent to which the myths about their relationships overflow with manifestations of the human shadow—lust, greed, jealousy, narcissism, infidelity, to mention just a few. The occasional inspirational love story is lost in the shuffle.

While these stories may shed light on the archetypal nature of the human condition, they tend to support the impossibility of conscious partnership rather than inspire the search for it. The Greek gods thrived on drama and their stories serve primarily to help us understand the more egoistic, secular stage of relationship.

So we turned our attention to Eastern traditions. Hindu theology, while still paternalistic at heart, does recognize the feminine as divine. However, the images are usually of a solitary mother goddess, such as Kali. There are several famous Hindu deity couples—Shiva/Parvati or Shiva/Shakti, and Krishna/Radha, to name a few. Still, only the stories of the former pair convey a true equality of empowerment and, even then, Shakti is generally depicted more as mother goddess and universal feminine principle than as spouse or lover.

We have long enjoyed the tale of Satyavan and Savitri from the *Mahabharata*, which reveals how conjugal love can conquer death.[1] Satyavan is the soul that carries the divine truth of being, who descends into the grip of death and ignorance. Savitri is the divine word, daughter of the sun, goddess of the supreme truth, who is given physical form to save Satyavan. Their story embodies the human struggle to find the way from our ordinary mortal state to divine consciousness and immortal life.

The story of Satyavan and Savitri is unusual. By and large, the more well-known Hindu deities are often solitary figures or the females are shown as consorts, subordinate to the males. In any event, these figures seemed too specific, culturally and historically, to shed much light on our personal experiences in Third Presence.

The situation is not significantly different in traditional Buddhism. Since it started primarily as a monastic religion, female empowerment was slow in coming into Buddhist cultures. We could find no deity lovers or partners with whom to identify strongly. Tibetan Buddhism does focus strongly on the image of "Yab-Yum," which is ubiquitous in tanka art. As noted earlier, the Yab-Yum image represents the sacred marriage of skillful means and wisdom in Vajra Buddhism, and compassion and emptiness in Mahayana Buddhism. Thus this image refers more to the balancing of masculine and feminine principles in the spiritual quest of an individual than to a pair of lovers. Similarly, the great yin/yang image of China and the Izanagi/Izanami myth of Japan describe primordial male/female principles and do not seem directly accessible as models for erotic relationship.

We found a compelling ancestor of our image of the Divine Pair in the ancient Egyptian myth of Isis and Osiris, who were both brother and sister as well as husband and wife.[2] This powerful myth does contain great wisdom about the nature of relationship,

---

[1] We have read and reread Aurobindo's epic poem, inspired by this myth. See *Savitri*, Sri Aurobindo, Sri Aurobindo Trust, 1970 (first issued in 1951).
[2] *The Passion of Isis and Osiris: A Union of Two Souls*, Jean Houston, Ballantine Books, 1995.

inspired by the cyclical rhythms of nature (the flooding of the Nile). Whether consciously or not, Isis and Osiris probably have taken their rightful place in the recesses of our visionary imagination, along with aspects of other divine pairs in our cultural ancestry.

Ultimately, we realized that the archetype of the Divine Pair is at a unique stage in its recognition and evolution. The need for insight about relationship from the Imaginal Realm has never been greater. The empowerment of women, although still a distant goal in many parts of the world, is slowly becoming a reality in the West. Support for male/female balance in relationship is growing in our culture. We feel contemporary experience and visionary imagination are meant to play a central role in creating an evolved, transcultural image of the Divine Pair to inspire intimate partnership the world over.